GROWING TOGETHER

MARY WHITE

NAVPRESS
A MINISTRY OF THE NAVIGATORS
P.O. Box 6000, Colorado Springs, CO 80934

The Navigators is an international Christian organization. Jesus Christ gave his followers the Great Commission to go and make disciples (Matthew 28:19). The aim of The Navigators is to help fulfill that commission by multiplying laborers for Christ in every nation.

NavPress is the publishing ministry of The Navigators. NavPress publications are tools to help Christians grow. Although publications alone cannot make disciples or change lives, they can help believers learn biblical discipleship, and apply what they learn to their lives and ministries.

Library of Congress Catalog Card
Number: 85-60546
ISBN: 0-89109-484-9
14845

Fourth printing, 1985

(Originally published as *Successful Family Devotions.*)

Printed in the United States of America

To Jerry,
whose loving leadership
has stimulated
and sustained
our family devotions.

Contents

Foreword 7

1 Why Bother? 9

2 Foundation I — The Bible 20

3 Foundation II — Prayer 40

4 Scripture Memory 52

5 Music 62

6 Combining the Secular and the Sacred 73

7 Tots 88

8 Tweens 95

9 Teens 107

10 Special Occasions 117

11 Special Problems 125

12 Keys to Continuing 133

Foreword

"Daddy, are you God?" My friend is still haunted by his child's sincere question. No, little one, your daddy isn't God, but he greatly influences your concept of God.

In a child's mind, heavenly fathers and earthly fathers are often identical twins. Perhaps the greatest challenge of parenthood is to teach children the truth about God. Nothing in life is as important to a child's future as his view of God. It is life's single most determinative fact.

God established the home as the primary educational context in which children learn to know and love their heavenly Father. Moms and Dads, you're on! It's your ball game, your challenge, your opportunity, your responsibility. But how can you fulfill it? A healthy family altar is a major step in the right direction. Morning and evening for over twenty years my eight brothers and sisters and I met with our parents around God's word for instruction, fellowship, and worship. Add to this squirming mass two missionary children who lived with us, and one short of a dozen kids gathered for a family altar twice a day.

Was it worth it? Unquestionably it was the wisest investment my parents ever made. God has honored their commitment, their steadfastness, and their patience. The returns have been good. I treasure the memories.

Am I following my parents' example with my family? By all means. I, too, believe that life's most crucial curriculum is taught in the home. Unfortunately, for most Christian homes, the television is the family altar, the major tool for teaching values and principles of life. The results have been bad.

Where do you go from here? Read the book, thank God for Mary White's excellent insights, make some plans, and begin. The family you save may be your own.

Joseph C. Aldrich
President
Multnomah School of the Bible

1 *Why Bother?*

DINNER WAS FINISHED and the dishes pushed aside when Joe brought his Bible from under his chair. He glanced at his wife, Susan, with a look and sigh that meant, Let's try it again.

The children around the table groaned a concert of "Oh, no" followed by a solo, "Can we hurry, Dad? I just remembered I have to feed the goldfish."

"Now listen, everybody," Joe said. "I'm going to read about Christ's triumphal entry into Jerusalem."

Four-year-old Alisa frowned in a puzzled way, then turned her attention to the dog waiting hopefully by her chair for an occasional bread crumb.

Joe read the account of Jesus' journey to Jerusalem recorded in John 12.

"Now," he said when he had finished, "let's have some questions. Peter, what did the crowds shout when they saw Jesus riding by?"

Peter, whose mind had no doubt been concentrating on his starving fish, looked blank and finally said, "Dunno, Dad."

Eight-year-old Danny just couldn't remember either.

In an attempt to receive some response, Joe turned to Alisa and asked, "Honey, what did Jesus ride on when he went to Jerusalem?"

Alisa puckered her little mouth in concentration and finally said tentatively, "On a cloud?"

Joe sighed, looked at Susan, and then said, "Well, we didn't do too well, kids. We'll try again tomorrow. You've got to listen better. Let's pray."

He prayed for about five minutes while the children fidgeted and twisted on their chairs. At one point Danny plopped softly on the floor, assisted there by a shove from his older brother. And Alisa, a moment later, whispered loudly, "Mommy, Peter's eyes are open."

When Joe finished praying, he asked what song the children would like to sing. Alisa said immediately, "I like 'Ornery Christian Soldiers'."

After singing one verse of the song, in which Joe and Susan made the only audible contribution, the children tumbled from their chairs and raced away. Joe gave Susan a rueful grin and shrugged his shoulders.

Joe and Susan represent many Christian parents who feel an honest desire to convey spiritual truth to their children, but find their attempts failing and falling short of their expectations. After a period of discouragement, they either forge ahead and continue with family devotions that are boring, tedious, and unproductive, or they abandon the whole idea and rationalize that their children rarely miss Sunday school, so surely they are receiving good teaching. Anyway, they have Bible story books to look at when they go to bed at night so that, too, will be of some help.

James and Judy Baxter have four children, ages three, seven, and twelve (twins). Three years ago the Baxter's neighbors talked to them one night about their need to receive Christ. James and Judy had never heard the plan of salvation before, but they were convinced they needed Christ, and that evening made the decision to become Christians. Their neighbors then urged them to read the Bible and pray in order to "grow."

James and Judy didn't understand why reading the Bible and praying were important, but they began to do it every evening and soon discovered the joy of finding truths in God's word, and the deep satisfaction of a two-way communication with God.

Deeply committed to their new life, they tried to communicate their experience to their children. Every evening after dinner, James read a chapter of the Bible to his family and then prayed aloud. But the children didn't respond. Rather, they were bored, kicked one another under the table, and complained.

Hurt and baffled by the children's reactions, James and Judy sought help. The neighbors who led them to Christ had no children and could think of no suggestions. James and Judy asked parents in the church they attended. Typical responses were:

- Do it even if the kids don't like it. It's good for them whether they know it or not.
- Try it just on Sunday. They expect it then.
- Why bother? They can start that when they grow up.
- Buy a Bible story book with pictures.
- Forget it. I tried it and it's hopeless.
- We know it's important, but we've never gotten around to it with our own children. We're so busy, you know.

The Baxters struggled on for a while, but by the time the twins were twelve they had abandoned the idea.

Because the church James and Judy attended was large, they never met Anne, a widowed mother of three children. She could have given them many clues to success. A look into her home during breakfast would have revealed a Bible-centered family time filled with animated discussions, questions, sincere prayers, laughter, and sometimes sympathetic tears.

One morning Anne brought three small packages to the breakfast table and placed them by the salt and pepper. They remained there until breakfast was over and then Anne said, "In place of Bible reading this morning, I'm offering a surprise reward to anyone who can accurately quote a Bible verse we learned last month and tell us what it means. You have one minute to pick a verse and review it to yourself."

Her children concentrated fiercely for one minute and then each managed to quote a verse and give an explanation. Because one of the children hesitated, Anne later jotted his verse on a little card and slipped it into his school lunch box.

Then Anne brought out a picture album of close family friends. Each child picked one person to pray for.

Finally, Anne led them to a kitchen counter where she had placed small clay pots, seeds, and soil. The children planted the seeds, watered them, and put the pots in a window. In several weeks the growing plants would be ready to offer as Christmas gifts. While they worked they talked about the joys of giving.

All of these activities took about twelve minutes and the children were attentive for the entire time.

What made the difference between the devotions in Anne's home and those in the Baxter's? Why did one home experience lively, memorable devotional times while the other family failed miserably? Simply stated, the Baxters began properly, with correct motives, but they lacked the ideas to make the time meaningful and relevant to their children. Anne gave more thought and preparation to the time she spent with her children.

The Bible gives us ample motivation for teaching our children spiritual truth. Hebrew parents were urged to make the law of God a very natural and constant part of family life. Deuteronomy 6:4-7 describes the spontaneous and normal approach to passing truth on to the next generation.

> Hear, O Israel: The Lord our God, the Lord is one. Love the Lord your God with all your heart and with all your soul and with all your strength. These commandments that I give you today are to be upon your hearts. Impress them on your children. Talk about them when you sit at home and when you walk along the road, when you lie down and when you get up.

In Christian homes the words of God should be discussed and repeated as naturally and as often as we would comment on the weather, but with infinitely more importance. Talking of spiritual things should be vital, but not stilted; natural, but not frivolous; frequent, but not tedious.

When we discuss the things of God with our children, they should sense their importance and significance to us. If we do not experience the significance of Scripture and prayer, we cannot possibly communicate that to our children. They will intuitively detect the hypocrisy and reject our efforts to lead them in a devotional time, or any exchange of spiritual ideas. If we suddenly adopt a preachy or solemn tone of voice, children will toss up a barrier that we cannot penetrate.

Family devotions are the formalized, structured times of ongoing teaching and communication—a time when parents and children alike can count on group sharing, learning, and worship. Not all spiritual teaching and communication will take place during devotions. Certainly we will want to be looking for opportunities to talk about the Lord and the relevance of Scripture to our daily lives. We will want to teach our children to pray spontaneously in many situations. But the devotional time can be used as a base, a foundation for the teaching that stimulates their own spiritual growth.

The apostle Paul gave one family special approval for their success in passing spiritual truth and values from one generation to the next. Writing to Timothy, Paul reminds him of the source of his faith. "I have been reminded of your sincere faith, which first lived in your grandmother Lois and in your mother Eunice and, I am persuaded, now lives in you also" (2 Timothy 1:5).

Timothy grew to manhood under the spiritual influence and tutoring of his mother and grandmother. They carried on this teaching even under the handicap of what was likely an unbelieving Greek father. No doubt, Lois had given Eunice a strong, lasting faith which they then colabored to impart to Timothy. And of this spiritually well-grounded man, Paul said,

> If Timothy comes, see to it that he has nothing to fear while he is with you, for he is carrying on the work of the Lord, just as I am (1 Corinthians 16:10).
>
> I hope in the Lord Jesus to send Timothy to you soon, that I also may be cheered when I receive news about you. I have no one else like him, who takes a genuine interest in your welfare (Philippians 2:19-20).

Paul relied heavily on Timothy, whose Christian faith and

growth were established when Paul met him, thanks to the consistent teaching of two women who obeyed God. Years of devoted, conscientious teaching paid off. Timothy's faith and faithfulness were recorded both in Scripture and in the lives of those to whom he ministered. As Paul's closest friend and associate, Timothy filled a large role in pastoring the early church.

Psalm 78 emphasizes the importance of teaching our children.

> I will open my mouth in parables, I will utter things hidden from of old—things we have heard and known, things our fathers have told us. We will not hide them from their children; we will tell the next generation the praiseworthy deeds of the Lord, his power, and the wonders he has done. . . . so the next generation would know them, even the children yet to be born, and they in turn would tell their children. Then they would put their trust in God and would not forget his deeds but would keep his commands (Psalm 78:2-4, 6-7).

In the opening chapters of Proverbs, King Solomon repeatedly calls his children to be attentive to his teaching, for through that instruction they will know the Lord.

> Listen, my son, to your father's instruction and do not forsake your mother's teaching (Proverbs 1:8).
>
> My son, if you accept my words and store up my commands within you . . . then you will understand the fear of the Lord and find the knowledge of God (Proverbs 2:1,5).
>
> Listen, my sons, to a father's instruction; pay attention and gain understanding (Proverbs 4:1).
>
> My son, pay attention to my wisdom, listen well to my words of insight (Proverbs 5:1).

Spiritual teaching is a constant, continuing process in the lives of our children, with the devotional time forming the base of communication. In a clearly worded statement, Paul reminds fathers of their responsibility to "bring them [their children] up in the training and instruction of the Lord" (Ephesians 6:4).

To "bring them up" is a long process from infancy to adulthood. Parents need conviction, stamina, creativity, and concern to spend years focusing on the spiritual welfare of their children. But God commands and expects this of parents.

Susanna Wesley, wife of Samuel Wesley and mother of the three famous Wesley brothers, Samuel, John, and Charles, gave birth to nineteen children and raised ten of them to maturity. She strongly felt the need to educate her children, and from an early age they were taught to read (an unusual practice with girls in eighteenth-century England). She regularly spent an hour with each child in concentrated spiritual discussions, and the family prayed together before the morning and evening meals. The influence of her efforts has been felt worldwide through the preaching and hymn writing of her sons.

My own father and mother led family devotions every morning and instilled in my brothers and sisters and me a reverence for the Bible, a confidence in prayer, and a desire for a close, personal relationship with God through Jesus Christ. During many of my growing years we lived on a farm, and having morning devotions meant that crucial work had to be postponed while my parents gave time to spiritual teaching. Field work waited, animals weren't fed, machines weren't fixed. All activities halted while we met as a family to worship and learn about God. Was it worth the effort it took to organize each day and set aside the time for devotions? Unquestionably, yes. Today my brothers and sisters and their children all love and serve God.

What are some specific motivations for having devotions?

- God commands parents to teach their children.
- Childhood is a prime time for learning. Children are open-minded and accepting of new stimuli and ideas. Parents are in an excellent position to select what will fill their minds.
- Parents can lead their own children to a personal relationship with God through Christ.

- Parents can disciple their own children—help them understand and develop attitudes and a lifestyle which are pleasing to God. Parents can introduce their children to the exciting adventure of a lifelong walk with God.
- Structured devotions provide a cohesive, spiritual center for a family. The family is the basic social unit in the Christian community. There we learn to relate as family members and as fellow Christians.

Unfortunately, some parents carry out family devotions with negative motivations that throw a gloomy atmosphere over what should be a joyous time. Several issues can make it a negative time.

- *Guilt*—The pastor said we had to do it . . . My sister's family does it, so I suppose we should . . . My folks always had devotions, so it must be the thing to do . . . All the other people in our Bible study group say they have devotions with their children.
- *Regret*—We've wasted ten years already since we had children. We had better get going. I guess it's now or never.
- *Legalism*—If we don't have family devotions, God will punish us . . . Since I sat through an hour's worth of devotions as a child, then my children must too.
- *Desperation*—Our teenagers are going wild. We've got to do something spiritual and see if that will help.
- *Authoritarianism*—My kids are going to listen and learn whether they like it or not. I know what's good for them even if they don't appreciate it.

Teaching our children is a privilege. But if our efforts are only supported by negative motivation, they become drudgery, a grind, and a failure. God wants parents to be convinced from his word that spiritual training is of utmost importance.

If you knew that your children would never have any source of spiritual truth other than yourself, would you panic? If all Sunday schools, Christian schools, Christian bookstores, gospel radio and television programs, and Christian literature were removed, how would you handle the spiritual training of your family? Would you plan and carry out the best possible family devotions?

We need to live as though we are the only available source of spiritual training for our children. God holds parents responsible for the training they receive. Many other inputs are excellent, but parents contribute the *primary* spiritual training in a child's life. How is it in your home? Do your children welcome family devotions? Are your attempts sporadic and weak? Have you tried, failed, and abandoned the attempt? Would you like to add spark to devotions?

All parents should take the time to think through and to write out on paper a description of the kind of adult they would like to see their child become. Such an exercise produces motivation for providing good spiritual training in the home. When you see what you would like your child to become, you can more easily plan how to structure your family devotional activities. Your description might look like this:

> I want my child to become a godly woman (or man) who knows Christ, applies the Bible to her (or his) life, prays in faith, has a concern for other Christians, is a courteous, decent, moral, wholesome human being, contributes to the body of Christ, and to society as a whole.

Finally, and most importantly, pray over every aspect of your children's spiritual training. When we have a goal to achieve, motivation, plans, and accomplishment fall more easily into place. Helping your child become a loving, responsible, godly man or woman will take years of concentrated, prayerful effort. There are no formulas for instant success. Parents need to make a commitment to God and to the child until the goal is achieved.

Recently I joined a panel presenting ideas, suggestions, and materials to use for family devotions. The interest, questions, and feedback from the audience indicated a desire to find real success in family devotions. Many people made comments that revealed common problems.

- My teenagers don't want to be bothered.
- Our family members have such busy schedules that we never seem to be together.
- I'd like to try some new things. What are some of the things I could do to make our family devotional time more interesting?
- My husband isn't interested. Should the children and I go ahead anyway?
- We have children ranging in age from four to sixteen. How do we interest everyone?
- How spiritual and serious should the devotions be?
- Do they have to be daily?
- How long should devotions be?
- Should we ever add other things, or should everything be spiritual?
- Should we force our children to pray aloud?
- Do children have to close their eyes when they pray?

Many parents do not lead the family in devotions because they do not have personal devotions themselves. Before you try family devotions, begin a daily time of personal devotions. The habit we wish to build into our children is daily Bible reading and prayer. But do you read your Bible daily and pray?

The saying, *Do as I say, not as I do* never works with children. They need to see and know that we spend time with God and that God has first place in our lives.

If you have never been personally successful in a daily time with God, try these suggestions.

1. Set aside ten to fifteen minutes at a specific time daily, perhaps before breakfast or bedtime.
2. Read a short passage from the Bible. Begin in the New Testament or the Psalms or Proverbs.
3. Meditate on (think over) what you have read, and select one thought to recall during the day.
4. Spend a few minutes praying about what you have read, your family, your work, and other items which concern you. Include a time of thanks and praise to God.

Even if it is done in the privacy of your room, your children will know if you spend personal time with God. Be an example. Lead them in the things of God. You will find your own life enriched as you pursue a program of personal devotions.

Why bother with family devotions? Because God wants parents to take the primary responsibility for leading family members to spiritual maturity. A few simple principles will make your family devotions creative times of mutual encouragement and spiritual growth. Leading your family in creative family devotions may be one of the most challenging and most rewarding adventures you ever have. Family devotions are well worth the bother!

2 Foundation I—The Bible

OUR CHILDREN WERE seated on the edges of their chairs, each child clutching a Bible. Their eyes were fixed on my face as I said, "Present arms, draw swords. John 15:7." Pause. "Charge!"

The children frantically flipped the pages of their Bibles, hoping to be the first to find the verse. After a moment Karen began reading aloud. "If you remain in me and my words remain in you, ask whatever you wish, and it will be given you."

On that particular evening we used twelve verses in our "sword drill." The children earned one point if they began reading the verse first, or two points if they correctly quoted it from memory. Some of the incentive for participating enthusiastically came from the prize in the center of the table, a coupon from me offering to be a substitute for the winner in dishwashing detail for the rest of the week.

We have made a strong effort to encourage our children to absorb the word of God into their lives. We use whatever means seems appropriate to help them use and appreciate the Bible. We believe that we must keep Scripture as one of the two basic essentials in our family devotions. The second essential is prayer. Although we enjoy variety and diversions during our devotional times, the Bible and prayer remain central.

Scripture remains the focal point in teaching our children the truths of God. When parents become convinced of that, family devotions become invigorating.

In this chapter, and the next, we will cover the two key elements of family devotions—Scripture and prayer. Other activities contribute and stimulate, but God has promised to bless his word, so it must remain the core of the devotional time. The word and prayer, presented in a positive, attractive way, allow parents to take the first steps in the process of directing their children into a lifelong relationship with God through Jesus Christ.

Through a gradual learning process, we have attempted to convey to our children God's reason for giving us the Bible as one of the key ways he has chosen to reveal himself to us. The Bible gives us insights into God's character and thoughts. Through Scripture we have the opportunity to know God in a living and intimate way.

Although the Bible is God's primary method of revealing himself, he is also known through other means.

The apostle Paul explains that God's natural creation reveals God to us. "For since the creation of the world God's invisible qualities—his eternal power and divine nature—have been clearly seen, being understood from what has been made, so that men are without excuse" (Romans 1:20).

The psalmist recognized this same truth when he wrote centuries earlier, "The heavens declare the glory of God; the skies proclaim the work of his hands" (Psalm 19:1).

When we see the grandeur of mountain peaks, or the pounding ocean surf, or a maple tree in glorious fall color, we are compelled to acknowledge the presence of a living, creative God.

God also uses the Holy Spirit to further reveal himself to us. Those who have believed in God through his Son Jesus Christ experience the comfort, help, and instruction of the indwelling Holy Spirit who reveals the things of God. "But God has revealed it to us by his Spirit. The Spirit searches all things, even the deep things of God. For who among men knows the thoughts of a man except the man's spirit within him? In the same way no one knows the thoughts of God except the Spirit of God" (I Corinthians 2:10-11).

Although God uses both nature and the Holy Spirit to reveal

himself, the chief tool the Holy Spirit uses to show us the mind of God is the Bible. In communicating God's truth to our children, we want to recognize all three sources, but place a special emphasis on the use of Scripture.

God could have chosen nature as the only way of knowing him, but instead he gave us the Bible, the only source document of his character and his relationship to man. Can we take this treasure lightly? Dare we allow our children to see that we do?

Because Bibles are so readily available in the United States today, we assume such widespread distribution is the norm. But only in recent centuries have Bibles been widely distributed, because of the invention of the movable type printing press.

The great breakthrough came in the 1400s with the invention of movable type by Johann Gutenberg. His greatest production was the famous Gutenberg Bible printed in 1456. This revolution, along with the translation of the Scriptures into the languages of the people by such men as Martin Luther and William Tyndale, paved the way for the common person to own a copy of the Bible in his own language.

Before that time, the Scripture was painstakingly copied by hand, and later by woodblock printing. Only a few people were privileged to possess a copy, and only rarely did a layman possess a Bible. Scripture was the guarded possession of the clergy. It was, in fact, believed that the common people had no right or ability to use and interpret the word of God.

Even today, however, Scripture has not yet been translated into every language. Only recently has the majority of people on earth been literate. Yet today millions of people still cannot read, and if they are to understand the gospel, someone must explain it to them orally.

In twentieth-century America, many different translations of the Bible are published. We have only to step into the nearest bookstore to make our choice. Sometimes the profusion of translations can cause some misunderstanding. When I taught sixth-grade girls in a Sunday school class, one of my students rushed into class the Sunday after Christmas waving a new Bible in her hand.

"Look, Mrs. White," she exclaimed. "My mom and dad gave me a new Bible for Christmas. It's the reversed version."

It took me a few moments to realize her parents had selected the *Revised Standard Version* for her.

If parents display indifference or ingratitude for the wonderful gift of Scripture, neither they nor their children will ever experience the joy of seeing God revealed in his word. Children will develop an appreciation for the Bible by observing their parents' attitude toward Scripture. We unconsciously, as well as deliberately, set a tone that our children will follow. This offers parents a special opportunity to influence their children's thinking about God's word.

We need to communicate to our children the great privilege of having the Bible in print and easily available. We should often mention that privilege and let our children know we are also fortunate to know how to read it.

Respect for God's Word

Our children will detect whether or not we treasure and highly honor the Bible. It is important for them to know that because Scripture relates God's tender expression of love and concern for us, we respect it above all other books and devote ourselves to obeying what it says.

When I was a girl, my parents suggested I should always keep my Bible on top of any stack of books and never cover it with my Sunday school papers, my hymn book, or my purse. It was a small gesture perhaps, but it made a lasting impression on me. The Bible deserved a place of esteem and honor and should never be lightly or carelessly treated.

Desire for God's Word

A desire for the word of God cannot be commanded or legislated. Children will learn to desire the word as they first observe their parents in concentrated reading, study, and application of the Bible, and then as they begin to hear and read it for themselves. Parents can convey their eagerness for the Bible by demonstrating a daily time of personal devotions and then verbally communicating enthusiasm for both private and family Bible reading.

My preschool niece lives nearby. When she comes to visit or stay with me, she will often get a Bible story book and bring it to me saying,

"*Read* to me, Auntie, *read* to me."

She has discovered in her own home the enjoyment of hearing the word of God, and she wants it to continue when she visits me.

The psalmist felt a desire for God's word when he wrote, "I delight in your decrees; I will not neglect your word" (Psalm 119:16).

A few months ago, Kathy, our college-age daughter, sat reading her Bible during a solitary early-morning breakfast. As I entered the kitchen she looked at me and said, "I just can't seem to get enough of the word these days, Mom. I just love to read the Bible."

Any parent would be pleased to hear a child make such a statement. And as God's children, surely his heart is delighted when we, as well as our children, can't "get enough of the word."

But suppose you don't feel that way, and you can't communicate that desire honestly to your children. Perhaps you feel "dry" when you read the Bible and try to concentrate on the things of God. The Lord knew of that feeling when he told Jeremiah regarding the returning Israelite exiles, "I will give them a heart to know me, that I am the Lord. They will be my people and I will be their God, for they will return to me with all their heart" (Jeremiah 24:7).

Desiring God's word is a two-way desire—God will provide the desire and we respond with an increased desire. We can trust God for the desire, and then respond accordingly.

The apostle Peter urges us to desire the word of God. "Like newborn babies, crave pure spiritual milk, so that by it you may grow up in your salvation" (I Peter 2:2).

Parents can help their children develop a desire, or craving, for the Bible by offering them frequent, delicious bites of Scripture.

Love for God's Word

"Oh, how I love your law! I meditate on it all day long" (Psalm 119:97). A love and desire for God's word go hand in hand. Love for the Bible expresses itself in time spent in reading, study, and meditation. We can't expect our children to delve deeply into God's word when they are tiny, but by positively presenting Scripture to them, we can establish a love that will develop and mature as they grow older.

The beginning of that love in our children's lives will come as they sense our love for Scripture. A child who awakens in the morning to find his dad reading his Bible knows the love and esteem his father holds for the Bible. Children who see their mother turn off the television and open her Bible realize her desire and love for Scripture. Actions communicate to children far more effectively than verbal teaching.

We can ask God to give our children a love for his word, and then teach them the Scriptures, but the foundational support for that love will be built as they observe our time spent in the Bible.

A dozen times in Psalm 119, the psalmist bursts out with an enthusiastic exclamation of his love for God's law. He overwhelmingly loves the book of God and can't restrain his expressions of love. That is the attitude we want to communicate.

> For I delight in your commandments because I love them. I reach out my hands for your commandments, which I love, and I meditate on your decrees (Psalm 119:47-48).
>
> Your promises have been thoroughly tested, and your servant loves them (Psalm 119:140).
>
> I obey your statutes, for I love them greatly (Psalm 119:167).

Belief in God's Word

When James was in sixth grade, his best friend invited him to church where he heard and believed the gospel. James's parents were indifferent toward spiritual things, but urged him to go with his friend on Sunday mornings for then they were assured of a quiet house.

James enjoyed his time at church. During Sunday school he played games, worked at crafts, and heard Bible stories. As he passed through high school, he dropped Sunday school attendance but continued to attend all the youth group's social functions. He heard the gospel every time he attended church, but no one helped him progress beyond that one basic truth of the spiritual life.

A few weeks after entering college he heard a professor remark, "I guess there are still a few Bible thumpers around who haven't progressed beyond the ancient myths, but I hope none of them are in this class."

James wanted to be sophisticated and open-minded. He pitted his baby faith against the professor's philosophies. His faith failed the test and slowly James drifted toward the brink of agnosticism.

James had never been encouraged to *believe* the Bible. His understanding of salvation was sincere and clear, but he had never been led to study and believe the Bible as the infallible, inspired word of God. If he had, his experience in college might have strengthened, instead of weakened his faith.

Building confidence in Scripture requires consistent, frequent discussion of the truth of the Bible and the fact that it is God's dependable, sure word. It means clearly pointing out its truth, and carefully raising and answering some of the problems children will encounter later regarding the reliability of the Bible. Sometime in life every person will hear attacks against the Bible, such as:

- The Bible is full of contradictions.
- You can't prove that Jesus rose from the dead.
- The Bible doesn't agree with history.
- The Bible is too narrow. You can't have fun if you believe the Bible.
- No thinking person would believe in miracles. Modern science shows us they couldn't happen.

Our children need preparation for attacks against the Bible.

And the best preparation we can give them is to encourage them to believe the Bible as God's eternal word.

The Scriptures detail God's character for us, and give us confidence in his love and plan for our lives. Without belief in the Bible, our love, respect, and desire for the Scriptures become sentimental and distorted.

Knowledge of God's Word

When we talk with children about the Bible, they often display their incomplete knowledge by giving amusing interpretations of various passages.

Danny asked his mother, "Mom, guess who wrote the Bible."

"Who?"

"God's spider men."

After further discussion his mother determined that Danny was on the right track, but hadn't yet made a distinction between God's "spider men" and God's "inspired men."

Little Sammy, after he heard of the creation of Adam, remarked, "That must have been a dusty job!"

After hearing the story of the good Samaritan, David stared thoughtfully into space for a while, and then asked, "Which half was dead?"

Part of the purpose of family devotions is to familiarize children with the facts of the Bible. Basic Bible knowledge includes many of the basic facts of Scripture that we often take for granted after reading the Bible for many years. Some of the facts children need to learn are:

- the two basic divisions of the Bible (Old and New Testaments)
- the order of the books in the Bible
- the history of the Old and New Testaments
- the division of the books into major groupings (law, history, etc.)
- the number of authors
- the length of time for writing the entire Bible
- the location of the major characters in the Bible
- an outline of Jesus' life on earth

- facts about God (his names, his character)
- geography of Palestine
- history of the early church

A detailed grasp of the facts of Scripture requires years of intensive reading and study, but children can comprehend an overview, a basic outline, of the Bible. Even that will take years for them, as you go over and over some of the same stories and facts and truths.

When one of our children was in third grade, I noticed that she lacked an understanding of many Bible facts. Perhaps we had neglected this, or perhaps she didn't listen attentively, but I knew she needed help.

I took out my flannelgraph stories and we began with Adam and progressed through the Old Testament. We covered creation, Noah, Abraham, Isaac, Jacob, and so on. She quickly picked up some basic facts and sorted out the order and importance of some Bible characters. She now has a new understanding of the placement of the books in the Bible and the basic theme of each book.

We parents can't expect Sunday school to provide all of the basic knowledge of Scripture that we want our children to have. Studying a subject for one hour a week will not give needed depth and factual knowledge. When we teach our children, we know just what they are learning. However, it takes time, much time, and children will not grasp everything in the first several years of learning.

When Isaiah was trying to emphasize his message, he wrote, "For precept must be upon precept, precept upon precept; line upon line, line upon line; here a little, and there a little" (Isaiah 28:10, KJV).

Comprehension and understanding come through small repeated doses. What is so important about the facts? The basic historical facts of the Bible form the foundation for knowing specific doctrine and Bible truths. A Christian is handicapped if he is unfamiliar with the basic history, names, and events in the Bible.

After facts come concepts, for faith is built on the concepts presented in the Bible.

Fact	*Concept*	*Faith*
Jesus died and rose from the dead.	God's sacrifice provides redemption and salvation.	Personal faith in Jesus Christ as Savior

Along with the facts, it is important that children be taught about the inspiration of Scripture. Today the Bible is readily attacked, lightly treated, and culturally interpreted. But the Bible must be revered and handled as the complete authoritative revelation of God. The apostle Peter emphasizes the authority of Scripture.

> We did not follow cleverly invented stories when we told you about the power and coming of our Lord Jesus Christ, but we were eyewitnesses of his majesty. For he received honor and glory from God the Father when the voice came to him from the Majestic Glory, saying, "This is my Son, whom I love; with him I am well pleased." We ourselves heard this voice that came from heaven when we were with him on the sacred mountain. And we have the word of the prophets made more certain, and you will do well to pay attention to it, as to a light shining in a dark place, until the day dawns and the morning star rises in your hearts. Above all, you must understand that no prophecy of Scripture came about by the prophet's own interpretation. For prophecy never had its origin in the will of man, but men spoke from God as they were carried along by the Holy Spirit (2 Peter 1:16-21).

Application of God's Word

Even when children are tiny, they can learn the importance of applying Scripture to their lives. *Application* is another term for obedience.

Parents should never use the Bible as a club or a threat, but rather in a loving way we should present the commands of Scripture we are to obey. The directives of Scripture give guidelines that will help us live a happier life, more pleasing to God.

Someone said that the Bible was not given to increase our knowledge, but to change our lives. We must lead our children in personalizing Scripture. We can teach many areas of life from the Bible, such as:

- honesty
- relating to others
- anger
- forgiveness
- morality
- work
- faithfulness
- keeping our word
- marriage
- family relationships

Rather than digging up appropriate verses to correct a child or to encourage a child, we need to teach the specific concepts earlier in life so we can simply refer back to them when problems arise. We can help our children find real answers from the Bible for real issues in their lives.

One of our children went through a period of fearfulness when she was ten years old. She feared separation from us, the dark, new situations, death, and any possible disaster. And she feared that maybe, just maybe, the Bible wasn't true, that God didn't love her and she had no hope of heaven.

She asked us, "What if the people who don't believe the Bible are right?"

Through that dark period of fear and doubt, we used Scripture over and over with her. We read and then reread 1 John 5. We used Scriptures that detailed God's power, his love, and his attitude toward fear. Together we memorized Isaiah 41:10 and 2 Timothy 1:7.

When she went to bed at night we used a tape recorder with Christian music and the Bible on tape to saturate her mind as she went to sleep. This process effectively diverted her mind from her fears and focused her thoughts on the Lord. Through this time, which lasted for several weeks, we prayed much, both with her and for her. Eventually she came through the crisis, stronger in faith and confident that God could erase her fears.

Although the principal theme of the Bible is God's revelation of himself and his plan for our salvation, the Scriptures impact on our lives in many ways. They are limitless in their variety and scope. Those who have only a scanty knowledge of the Bible say that it appears full of contradictions. Those who love and delve into the Bible recognize the vastness of its teaching and the depth of the wisdom it contains. Even the most intensive, dedicated Christian Bible scholar acknowledges that he will never fully understand the Bible. There will always be new depths to plumb and new heights to scale. And some things will remain forever shrouded.

"The secret things belong to the Lord our God, but the things revealed belong to us and to our children forever, that we may follow all the words of this law" (Deuteronomy 29:29).

Parents can help their children see and experience many of the broad facets of Scripture. We can teach them some of the ways God's word affects our lives.

It Is a Lamp

"Your word is a lamp to my feet and a light for my path" (Psalm 119:105).

God's word provides guidance for our everyday walk. Knowledge of the Scriptures gives us confidence about the right way to live and how to conduct the everyday affairs of life.

Light dispels darkness, shadows, and uncertainty. Light gives boldness and confidence. That is what the Bible does for us. We can rely on the light Scripture gives in otherwise dark circumstances and situations.

It Is a Guide

"The Lord will guide you always" (Isaiah 58:11).

Most Christians eagerly anticipate doing the will of God.

They appreciate any messages, seminars, or books that will give clues on finding God's will for their lives. We all desire God's will for schooling, marriage, career decisions, and career changes. It is important that we determine God's best for us in these matters, and help our children learn how to find God's will in the issues of life.

But sometimes we overlook obvious signals that God has given us. Scattered throughout Scripture are specific directives on God's will for us.

> To do your will, O my God, is my desire; your law is within my heart (Psalm 40:8).
>
> For my Father's will is that everyone who looks to the Son and believes in him shall have eternal life, and I will raise him up at the last day (John 6:40).
>
> Be very careful, then, how you live—not as unwise, but as wise, making the most of every opportunity, because the days are evil. Therefore do not be foolish, but understand what the Lord's will is (Ephesians 5:15-17).
>
> Give thanks in all circumstances, for this is God's will for you in Christ Jesus (1 Thessalonians 5:18).

The Bible is a guide, an outline, and a road map for our lives, leading us through the character development process that God has planned for us.

Our Western culture offers many opportunities for a wide range of choices in schooling, careers, and marriage. Perhaps that is why we often think in terms of God's will applying to major decisions and commitments of life.

But the Bible provides daily guidance for us in the areas of attitudes, relationships, and behavior. And to have this continuing guidance, we need to read God's word daily, and share these principles with our children as well. Although God certainly expects us to follow the guidance of his word and the counsel of godly Christians as we determine his will for us in major decisions, the Bible remains our guide for daily living.

It Is Food

"I can't believe how she's grown," says Aunt Martha of her favorite niece when she sees her after a year's absence. "She is getting so big!"

An average baby weighs seven pounds at birth. Within a year his weight has tripled and he has changed from a helpless, unfocusing, unresponsive newborn to a toddling, inquisitive, loving youngster.

And soon, to his parents' amazement, he is riding a tricycle, starting school, delivering newspapers, driving the car, dating, and graduating from high school.

Growth means to develop, thrive, increase, and mature. For growth, that newborn demands food. His body provides signals to call for food. He must have it to develop to his full potential. Lack of food means poor health, possibly death.

God has used the analogy of food and growth in Scripture to remind us that we cannot grow spiritually without a regular diet of the word of God. Nourishment assures growth. Without food we perish. Spiritually we are weak or failing without the food of the word of God. Scripture refers to itself as meat, milk, and bread:

> Like newborn babies, crave pure spiritual milk, so that by it you may grow up in your salvation (1 Peter 2:2).

> Anyone who lives on milk, being still an infant, is not acquainted with the teaching about righteousness. But solid food is for the mature, who by constant use have trained themselves to distinguish good from evil (Hebrews 5:13-14).

> Then Jesus declared, "I am the bread of life. He who comes to me will never go hungry, and he who believes in me will never be thirsty" (John 6:35).

Feeding on the word of God lays the foundation for growing spiritually into the mature believers that God wants us to be. Feeding our children establishes their spiritual growth patterns as well.

It Is a Tool

"The word of God is living and active. Sharper than any double-edged sword, it penetrates even to dividing soul and spirit, joints and marrow; it judges the thoughts and attitudes of the heart" (Hebrews 4:12).

God uses his word as a penetrating tool to carve into the life of a Christian and expose areas that are contrary to Scripture.

Cutting hurts, but that pain precedes healing and growth. God is in the process of doing whatever is necessary to cut away the useless, negative parts of our lives and characters. He does it by using his word like a knife to slice into our thoughts, desires, attitudes, and ambitions.

God does this for us and for our children. Many times we are never aware of the way God is using his word as we present it to our children.

When one of our daughters was about eleven years old, she heard a sermon from 1 Corinthians 12 emphasizing the importance for each Christian to know and use his spiritual gift. That Sunday evening when I went to her room to kiss her goodnight, I found her crying. When I tried to comfort her, she told me the reason for her tears.

"I don't know what my spiritual gift is, and the pastor said we all have one."

I assured her that as she matured and grew, God would give her abilities and interests that would indicate her particular spiritual gift.

God's word works as a life-changing tool in the life of every Christian. We must be careful to use the Bible as a basis for what we say when we counsel our children, rather than using our own opinions, the standards of our peers, or the expectations of our church group. One Scripture verse, accurately and wisely used, will penetrate, guide, and correct the life of a Christian.

The Bible expresses God's great, all-encompassing love for mankind. The Bible was written to describe God's love for all people and his redemptive plan that allows us to approach him as a loving father. Jesus' birth, life, death, and resurrection demonstrated that love in a way nothing else could.

Our children need to experience God's love as they face a hostile, harsh world. As parents, we love imperfectly. God's love accepts and comforts without reserve or criticism.

> I have loved you with an everlasting love; I have drawn you with loving-kindness (Jeremiah 31:3).

> This is how God showed his love among us; He sent his one and only Son into the world that we might live through him (1 John 4:9).

Some of the first words a child should hear from his Christian parents should be, "God loves you." They will not fully understand the concept of God's love, but can begin to believe the truth of the idea. Indeed, what adult can fully understand this? God's love can be accepted and treasured, but never completely analyzed.

The Bible is a collection of God's treasured wisdom, providing us with gems for everyday living. "Oh, the depth of the riches of the wisdom and knowledge of God! How unsearchable his judgments, and his paths beyond tracing out!" (Romans 11:33).

The Bible provides the plan for eternal life, it corrects us, it teaches us how to live, it encourages obedience, it gives instruction for cleansing from sin, it comforts us, and it reveals the mind of God.

What a marvelous legacy to leave to our children. If we can teach them to know, believe, and obey the word of God, we will have done more to insure their happiness and contentment in life than if we had given them an outstanding education, a fine environment, or any other secular advantage.

Children need not learn all of these things at once, but parents will be helped in remembering the broad, penetrating power of Scripture in the life of every Christian who believes, reads, and studies the word of God. We always need to be alert for new and interesting methods of presenting Bible facts and truths to our children.

Early in the history of The Navigators, the founder of the

organization, Dawson Trotman, devised an illustration which pictures our grasp of the word of God.

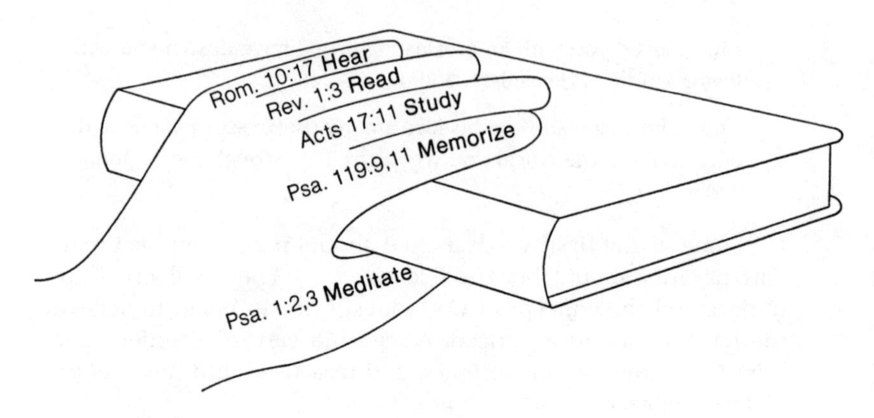

The Hand

The Hand shows us the five methods of learning from the Bible. Each of these methods is important.

Hearing the word from godly pastors and teachers provides us insight into others' study of the Scriptures as well as stimulating our own appetites for the word.

Reading the Bible gives us an overall picture of God's word. Many find helpful a daily reading program which takes them systematically through the Bible.

Studying the Scriptures leads us into personal discoveries of God's truths. Writing down these discoveries helps us organize and remember them better.

Memorizing God's word enables us to use the sword of the Spirit to overcome Satan and temptations . . . to have it readily available for witnessing or helping others with a "word in season."

Meditation is the thumb of the Hand, for it is used in conjunction with each of the other four methods. Only as we meditate on God's word—thinking of its meaning and application to our lives—will we discover its transforming power at work in us.

When all five processes are active, anyone can have a firm hold on Scripture. The four means of Scripture intake—hearing, reading, studying, and memorizing—are easily understood, even by children. Depth in the word comes from the meditation process. Simply stated, meditation is burning a truth deeply into the mind and turning it into action. Key elements of meditation are:

- *repetition*—engraving facts on the mind
- *visualization*—experientially understanding the facts
- *internalization*—making the truth personally meaningful
- *application*—using the truth to alter actions

Creative family devotions put strong emphasis on the meditation process. We repeat facts as we hear them, read them, and memorize them. We visualize facts through pictures, games, and other aids. We internalize truths through discussion. We apply truths by being involved in projects, giving our time and resources, and taking part in family activities. We lead our children in active, enjoyable meditation as we teach God's word from many vantage points. When children see, smell, hear, and feel the incredible events of Scripture, a deep permanent message from God is etched in their minds and lives.

Several of the processes in the Hand illustration can take place when the child is still very young. Hearing, studying, and memorizing can be part of his daily intake of Scripture before he learns to read. He may not "study" in the academic sense, but repeated, concentrated review of Scripture is, to a child, study. And memory for a child comes easily. Children quickly learn television commercials, songs, and poems, so why not Bible verses?

The key to helping children absorb Scripture is to present the Bible as attractively as possible in a way that will capture their imaginations and burrow into their memories.

Use a variety of methods and materials. Find a Bible story book that your family likes. We have found *Egermeier's Bible Story Book* to be detailed, accurate, and appealing.

After a child learns to read, he should have his own Bible.

When our children were small, we made frequent use of *The Living Bible.* We felt that this paraphrase by Ken Taylor vividly portrayed the events and truths of the Bible for our children.

Visual aids help us teach biblical facts. Use flannelgraph materials, readily available at any Christian bookstore, or make your own. Use pictures—buy them, or save them from your children's Sunday school papers. Have your children draw as you read to them. Use puppets to tell a story. Try quiz cards, simple tests, role playing, Bible charades, and sword drills. Listen to a tape of Scripture. Develop whatever methods *your* family enjoys. Though you will find *reading* the Bible will be your primary means of learning Scripture, supplement it often with varied activities.

Give your children the great and lasting heritage of a love for Scripture, and a desire to obey what it teaches. Above all, demonstrate your own love for the Bible by reading it often and by practicing its teachings in daily living.

Suggested Resources

Bible Story Books

Egermeier, Elsie. *Egermeier's Favorite Bible Stories.* Anderson, Indiana: Warner Press, 1979.

——. *Egermeier's Bible Story Book.* New ed. Anderson, Indiana: Warner Press, 1979.

Taylor, Kenneth. *Living Bible Storybook.* Wheaton, Illinois: Tyndale House Publishers, Inc., 1970.

Suggested Bible Translations

The Living Bible, Paraphrased. Wheaton, Illinois: Tyndale House Publishers, Inc., 1971.

New American Standard Bible. Carol Stream, Illinois: Creation House, Inc., 1960.

New International Version of the Holy Bible. Grand Rapids, Michigan: Zondervan Bible Publishers, 1978.

3 Foundation II—Prayer

A FEW YEARS ago our aged family pet, a beagle named Pepi, developed an enormous tumor behind one eye. Because of her age and condition, surgery was not a realistic option. After many tears and loving final pats, the children let me lead her out the door for her last trip to the veterinarian's office where she was humanely put to sleep.

Our youngest child, eight years old at the time, desperately missed the dog, as did the rest of us, but her pain seemed especially severe. After a few weeks she began to talk of getting another dog. Her aunt had given her a picture book of dogs and she began to pour over it, studying each picture with interest.

One evening as I prayed with her, I heard her say, "Dear God, please let me have a German shepherd dog."

A German shepherd! Wait, Lord. Listen to me before you answer her prayer, I thought. *A German shepherd! Isn't that one of those fierce beasts with bared fangs and a killer instinct? How about something smaller, say a Pekinese, instead?*

But Kristin continued to pray daily for a German shepherd. And she was confident God would bring her one.

A few months later our son called from Colorado. "Mom, I've found a German shepherd puppy abandoned by the road. He's such a nice dog, but I can't keep him where I live. Would you take him? I really don't want to have him destroyed."

Could this be God's answer to Kristin's prayer? But an abandoned dog? What was the matter with him? How could we transport him from Colorado to Washington? Several phone calls later, we agreed to pick up the dog on a trip to Colorado.

Kristin was jubilant at God's answer. She loves her dog and has brought him from a cowering, cringing, fearful state to one of boisterous, playful confidence. Many times we have heard her thank God for her dog.

Does God hear our children pray? Of course. God wants to hear our children pray. Jesus said, "Let the little children come to me, and do not hinder them, for the kingdom of heaven belongs to such as these" (Matthew 19:14).

Have you ever considered why God allows us to pray to him? Why didn't he just give us the Bible and tell us about himself and his plan for us? God wants a relationship with us. If he only spoke to us through his word, we would never know the privilege of two-way communication through the word and prayer.

Actually, the word *communication* fails to express adequately what takes place in prayer. *Communion* describes it much better. Communication involves the exchange of facts and knowledge, but communion implies an intimate union with deep understanding, a sharing of emotions and thoughts.

God has opened to us the privilege of prayer with himself. We do our children a great service when we teach and encourage them to pray about everything. "Do not be anxious about anything, but in everything, by prayer and petition, with thanksgiving, present your requests to God" (Philippians 4:6).

Prayer replaces anxiety. Prayer precedes peace. Do your children seem apprehensive, given to worry, fearful? Teach them to pray—about everything. Let them know that God is interested and will hear anything they want to say.

As you listen to your children pray, you will hear almost anything, even amusing statements like:

- Dear Jesus, thank you for dying on the cross for me. Thank you for forgiving my sins—I forgive you of yours.
- Thank you, Jesus, that you are President over all.
- Dear God, I have a cold. Please make my nostrils work.

Though amusing to us, children are completely serious when they pray. God knows what they mean and he hears them. Younger children will pray with complete candor about everything, often confusing doctrinal issues, but approaching God with faith and confidence. As children grow, they develop a more selective approach to prayer, but parents can help them retain that complete assurance that God is interested in everything they have to say.

You will hear, through your children's prayers, many things that you had not previously realized concerned them.

When our son was small, he never expressed interest in his sister's appearance, but when she was eight months old, we heard him pray, "God, please make her hair grow."

The growth of the baby's hair wasn't the main factor of interest to us as Steve's parents. We realized, as he prayed, that he had a concern for his sister and faith that God would respond to the need.

As your children grow older and you share times of open family prayer, you will hear many statements that will allow you insight into their thinking, their needs, their pressures and joys. You might hear:

- Dear God, please help my friend Brian whose parents are getting a divorce.
- Thank you, Lord, that I passed the history test.
- Give me courage to witness to my friend.
- Please help me pass my driving test.
- Thank you, God, for loving me even when I fail to love you back.
- Lord, would you give our family another baby?
- Please help our team to win the soccer game.

But remember that we don't teach our children to pray so that we can gain insights into their lives, but so they will know how to communicate with God, *their* heavenly Father.

What should we teach them regarding prayer? We have found the "ACTS" method of prayer helpful in teaching our children the basic elements of prayer outlined in Scripture.

A—Adoration
C—Confession
T—Thanksgiving
S—Supplication

Adoration. The word *adore,* or *adoration,* is not found in the Bible, but the concept of adoration clearly comes through in all of Scripture. It is closely related to the concept of praise.

Adoration implies love, worship, admiration, reverence, and respect. God is worthy of all of these feelings from us.

When we teach our children to praise God, we teach them adoration.

> I will extol the Lord at all times; his praise will always be on my lips (Psalm 34:1).
>
> Through Jesus, therefore, let us continually offer to God a sacrifice of praise—the fruit of lips that confess his name (Hebrews 13:15).
>
> Because your love is better than life, my lips will glorify you (Psalm 63:3).

Praise God for who he is, and for what he has done. True praise is expressed simply. Even very young children can praise and adore the Lord in simple terms.

- Thank you that you are love.
- I praise you for being kind.
- Praise you for sending Jesus to die for my sins.
- I thank you for making the world.

Praise turns our thoughts from ourselves to focus on God. Praise gives us an opportunity to remember with gratitude and awe who God is. The better we know God and his word, the more we will have to praise him for.

As we teach our children from Scripture, we can show them how to praise God. When we read the story of Moses leading the nation of Israel, we can direct their thoughts to praise for God's control over nature, his love, his protection, and his care for his people.

Include praise daily in prayer times with your children. Use the word *praise* several times as you pray and your children will understand that praise is an integral part of knowing God. Read through a psalm with them as a praise prayer, such as Psalm 95 or Psalm 100.

Confession. As a Christian, one of the most dreadful inner conflicts we can suffer is guilt. Anytime we violate the rules of God, we experience guilt. Our children experience it as well. God knew our need to be free of the guilt of our sin and he provided the means of confession.

Confession involves acknowledging and admitting wrong, then believing and accepting God's forgiveness. "If we confess our sins, he is faithful and just and will forgive us our sins and purify us from all unrighteousness" (1 John 1:9).

The psalmist understood the need for confession when he wrote, "Then I acknowledged my sin to you and did not cover up my iniquity. I said, 'I will confess my transgressions to the Lord'—and you forgave the guilt of my sin" (Psalm 32:5).

Confession leads to freedom and restoration. Unconfessed sin weighs heavily on the conscience. But confessed sin is a prelude to joy and liberty.

The Scripture records a time of national confession in Israel. The entire nation gathered after the wall around Jerusalem was rebuilt under the leadership of Nehemiah. For several days they read the law and then prayed and confessed their sins. After prayer and confession, they proceeded with much jubilation to rededicate the wall they had rebuilt (see Nehemiah 1-10).

Confession should be made daily. Children need to keep short accounts with God, and the younger they are, the more immediate the confession needs to be. We can help them confess their sin several times a day if that seems appropriate.

Have they shouted unkind words to another family member?

Teach them that such behavior offends God who commands us to "be kind and compassionate" (Ephesians 4:32). Pray with them, also letting them say, "I'm sorry that I talked mean to my sister."

A key factor in confession is God's promise that he forgives and forgets our sins. "As far as the east is from the west, so far has he removed our transgressions from us" (Psalm 103:12).

We don't need to review and mull over our past sins. They have been forgiven by God and removed from us and from his memory. If we can communicate that truth to our children and help them accept and believe it, their lives will take on a freedom unknown to those who carry a load of guilt.

But parents must allow children to forget. If they have confessed their sin, we cannot resurrect that offense. Even if they repeat, we must deal with the present problem, not past mistakes, for those have been forgiven and forgotten by God.

Thanksgiving. Praise and thanksgiving blend so closely they are often difficult to distinguish. Praise focuses more on the person of God, while thanksgiving centers on what he has done for us. The distinctions mellow and blend together during prayer. Both praise and thanksgiving please and honor God. Both are significant elements in our prayer life.

Thanksgiving during prayer provides a positive approach to God's dealings in our lives, as well as a positive outlook on life in general.

Children need to concentrate on God's goodness to them and on the truth that "all things work together for good" (Romans 8:28, KJV).

Expressing our thanksgiving must be of great importance to God, for he includes it as part of his direct will for our lives. "Give thanks in all circumstances, for this is God's will for you in Christ Jesus" (1 Thessalonians 5:18).

If we are practicing a consistent pattern of thankful thinking, all our circumstances will prove much more pleasant and enjoyable.

When children learn to be thankful in prayer, they can more clearly recognize the goodness, the omnipotence, the loving care of a heavenly Father. A thankful spirit in prayer will spill over into daily living and help them be more positive, thankful, happy people.

Tiny children must be taught to thank God for many things, but they will soon grasp the idea. When our son was small, we were trying to teach him to thank God in everything. Soon he grasped the idea and would begin his prayer time by saying, "Thank you God for EVERYTHING." Then he would proceed to enumerate each family member, all his friends, his distant acquaintances and, finally, when he began to run out of items he would open one eye, glance around, close it again and say, "thank you for the curtains." The eye would open again and close so that he could say, "Thank you for the walls." The process would go on for some time until he exhausted all the items in visual range. We did not discourage him from this rather tedious procedure for we knew that he was building patterns for a thankful spirit.

When you listen to your children pray, you can determine certain needs in their relationship with God. And if you rarely hear them express thanks, you know that they need to begin to include that in their thinking and their prayers. A lack of thanksgiving can stem from bitterness, selfishness, or simply a failure to understand that God is the source of all things. "Every good and perfect gift is from above, coming down from the Father of the heavenly lights, who does not change like shifting shadows" (James 1:17).

Always emphasize to your children that when they pray *for* something and God answers, they should thank God specifically for that answer. It will increase their faith and impress them with the fact that God wants to hear us express our appreciation for his goodness.

Supplication. Supplication involves two aspects of asking God for something—prayer for others and prayer for ourselves. When children are young, supplication forms the largest part of their prayers. Until they develop a deeper understanding of God's role in their lives, they tend to view God as a "goodie giver." They feel if they just ask God for something, it will certainly be forthcoming.

We can help our children understand that God desires to

hear their prayers and to respond to their needs. And they can learn that one of the great privileges in the Christian community is praying for others and their needs. "If you remain in me and my words remain in you, ask whatever you wish, and it will be given you" (John 15:7).

God openly invites us to pray to him regarding anything in our lives. The redemptive work of Christ made prayer to God possible. We can teach our children to take advantage of God's generous invitation to bring our prayers to him.

Practical Helps

We want our children to learn the meaning of 1 Thessalonians 5:17, which teaches us to "pray continually." Prayer is an attitude of the mind. For the Christian who walks with God, prayer should come as an automatic response to every situation.

Recently I was driving with a friend on a busy freeway. Suddenly we came upon an accident. It had just happened, because dust was still flying in the air. Several cars had stopped to help, so we proceeded cautiously. As we passed the demolished car, my friend began praying aloud for the people in the car, their recovery, and the help that was coming to them.

My friend's response demonstrates the attitude we want to instill in our children, that whatever their circumstances—sad, troubled, or joyful—they will respond to God in prayer. They need not pray audibly, but with inner, thankful, petitioning prayer.

There are several suggestions we can follow in helping our children make prayer an integral part of their lives.

Set an example. When you pray with a small child, pray simply so that he can pray as you do. Use short sentences and simple words such as, "Thank you for Jesus," "Bless my teacher," and "Help grandma get well."

As children mature they can learn to use more complicated words and sentences. The Lord isn't interested in flowery speech, but rather sincere prayer from the heart.

When praying with older children or teens, lead them by example in what you pray for and how you give thanks and praise.

They will follow an example of prayer much more easily than they will be able to apply teaching about prayer.

When Jesus' disciples asked him for teaching on prayer, he didn't go into a long discourse, but rather he prayed and gave them an example to follow.

Never, never criticize your child's prayers. They are not praying to you, but to God the loving, heavenly Father. If you criticize their grammar or the content of their prayers, you may raise barriers that will be difficult to break down. Allow your child to express himself freely to God, and continue to lead him by example. He will learn to pray as you set a good example, but if he is criticized, he may regard prayer from a negative perspective. As he grows older he will abandon any attempt to pray, feeling that either you or God will not find his prayers acceptable.

Never insist that your children pray aloud. You may find an exception to this rule, but it would indeed be rare. Children, and especially teenagers, may go through periods when they are hesitant or shy about praying in front of others. Offer them the opportunity, but if they refuse, don't insist. Again, they aren't praying to you or for you, but to their heavenly Father, and if they do so under duress from parents, prayer becomes a futile exercise.

Be patient with them and eventually they will once again be willing to participate aloud in prayer. It may take weeks or even months, and you may feel the spiritual life has disappeared, but don't lose heart. Encourage them from time-to-time to pray in the privacy of their rooms, and eventually they will rejoin the family in audible prayers.

Use conversational prayer. Let each member of the family pray a sentence, then stop and allow someone else to pray. This method is helpful to use with a family as it allows every member to participate and yet the prayers aren't lengthy. Children feel pressured when they feel required to pray at length about many items. They feel unable to remember enough items to pray about.

Conversational prayer allows the parent to guide the prayers, yet each member can participate freely. A typical time of conversational prayer might sound like this:

Mom: We praise you, Lord, that you are love.
Dad: Father, we praise you for creating all things.
Jim: Praise you for making trees.
Jan: Thank you, Father, for my family.
Dad: Thank you for this new day and the beautiful weather.
Jim: Thank you for my friends.
Mom: Father, please help us to love you more today.
Jan: Help my teacher to get well.
Jim: Please help my friend Sam become a Christian.
Jan: Help me with my history test.
Dad: Thank you that the children have a good school to go to.

Conversational prayer can be extended for many minutes, or shortened to include just a few items and a few members of the family. Conversational prayer may concentrate on only one aspect of prayer, perhaps thanksgiving, or petition, or it may include all aspects. Parents can lead children from one area to another by introducing new topics into the prayer time and allowing the children to follow with items of their own.

Vary positions as you pray. The Bible speaks of kneeling, standing, sitting, lying down, and walking as possible positions for prayer. Variety helps children understand that no matter where they are, they can pray. One day after reading Scripture in your devotional time, go outside and walk, praying conversationally as you go. Or kneel together around the dinner table. Or sit on the floor in a circle, holding hands as you pray.

Use lists and pictures. Teach your children to keep prayer lists by maintaining a family prayer list. Jot down in a notebook items to be thankful for and requests for the family and other people that you know. When you hear of a response or answer from God, jot that in the notebook by the request. Your children will see firm evidence that God answers prayer.

If your family knows some missionaries well, make them a specific subject of your prayers. When their letters arrive, record in your notebook specific requests they ask you to pray about and then pray over those requests with your children. When the next letter arrives, check to see which of those prayers have been answered.

Keep a photo album of people you pray for—missionaries, family members, and friends. Pass the photos around as you pray for different ones to remind your children who they are. This is especially helpful if you live some distance from family members. Younger children need a point of reference for their prayers.

When I was a little girl, our family prayed for a single woman who was a missionary in China. We knew what she looked like because we had her picture available. As children we were consistent in our prayers for her spiritual work. My younger brother became so fervent in his prayer for her one day that he prayed that she "wouldn't spread out the gospel too thin."

Teach your children to pray BIG to increase their faith. When they pray for things that seem impossible from their point of view and find that God answers, their faith is given a tremendous boost.

Teach them to pray about every detail of life which concerns them.

Teach them to wait for answers from God.

Teach them to pray for those things the Scripture specifically instructs us to pray for:

- laborers for the harvest
- our enemies
- our rulers
- our fellow Christians
- our daily bread

When we teach our children to pray and regularly lead them in prayer, we are building a foundation in their spiritual lives that will last and support them for a lifetime.

Suggested Resources

Rinker, Rosalind. *Prayer: Conversing with God.* Grand Rapids, Michigan: Zondervan Publishing House, 1959.

4 *Scripture Memory*

WHEN KRISTIN WAS eight years old, she was sitting beside me in church one Sunday morning. The pastor moved to the pulpit to read the Scripture portion. As he began, Kristin nudged me with her elbow and grinned. He was reading Isaiah 41:10, the verse that Kristin had just finished memorizing. I watched her mouth the words along with his reading, proof that the verse was embedded in her mind.

The most precious heritage you can give your children, apart from leading them to Christ, is Scripture, deeply imprinted in their memories, ready to be recalled at anytime throughout life. Children who have consistently memorized Scripture will find it springs to the forefront of their minds at just the right time for praise, for encouragement, and as a deterrent to sin.

Children should start a pattern of memorizing God's word before they realize that, although it is the *normal* thing to do in the Christian life, it is not the *average* thing to do. Few, very few, professing adult Christians regularly memorize Scripture. Rather, they consider memory work a Sunday school activity or they decide their brains are past the age of memorization.

Scripture memory activities fade after the elementary school years. Several organizations offer programs to help with Bible memory, but enrollment in these plans indicates only a small percentage of the millions of professing Christians consistently memorize Scripture successfully.

Memorizing Scripture with your children will renew this enjoyable and profitable exercise in the Christian life. Hopefully, memorizing Scripture as a family will establish an example that your children will follow when they are on their own spiritually.

Scripture gives ample indication that we should memorize the word of God.

It will protect us from sin. "How can a young man keep his way pure? By living according to your word. . . . I have hidden your word in my heart that I might not sin against you" (Psalm 119:9-11).

Are you concerned for the moral purity of your children? Do you worry as they find playmates and companions who have never received Christ? Do you detect traits of sin in their lives? Do they associate with other children who have no concept of the standards the Bible teaches? Teach them to memorize Scripture to protect them against the attacks of Satan that inevitably strike them during childhood and the vulnerable teen years.

The word of God implanted in their minds will rise to convict and deter your children from sin when the temptation comes. If they do succumb, Scripture will be there to convict and restore them to fellowship with God once again.

James grew up in a home where he regularly memorized Bible passages. When he was a teenager, he and several friends drove to a nearby town one evening. James had told his parents he needed the car to take his friends to a basketball game, but instead they joined a party complete with liquor and marijuana.

James had enough presence of mind to start for home about the time he had told his parents he would return, but his friends refused to leave. James drove home alone.

He mumbled "Good night" to his parents as he came in from the garage and headed for his room. He didn't notice the look his parents exchanged at the sight of his rumpled clothes and drawn face.

For the next two days James was progressively more quiet until the evening of the second day when he burst out, "Mom, Dad, I've got to tell you something. Neil and Joe and I went to a party the other night—a party I know you wouldn't have liked."

"We know, James," said his mother. "Neil's dad called us the next day. Neil and Joe didn't get home until 5 A.M."

"I know. They had somebody at the party bring them home. Now they're both mad."

"What made you decide to tell us this, Son?" asked his father.

"Well, Dad, I know it might sound kind of funny, but remember that verse we memorized a long time ago? 'Keep your tongue from evil and your lips from speaking lies.' That's just been pounding in my head these last couple of days and I just had to tell you. I couldn't live with it anymore."

The Holy Spirit will use memorized Scripture to bring our children to a realization of sin in their lives.

We can meditate on it. "Blessed is the man who does not walk in the counsel of the wicked or stand in the way of sinners or sit in the seat of mockers. But his delight is in the law of the Lord, and on his law he meditates day and night" (Psalm 1:1-2).

What do your children think about? You should be able to tell by the things they talk about. Do they refer constantly to the television programs they watch? Do they have a complaining, negative attitude? Do they express fear frequently? Or anger, or hostility, or excessive timidity?

Many of those characteristics develop as part of a child's personality, but planting Scripture in their minds will help them cultivate new patterns of thinking.

Your children may not be aware that they are *meditating,* but memorized material revives quickly in the mind, and memorized Scripture is always available for the Holy Spirit to use in correcting or encouraging your children.

Young children will not consciously meditate in a deep way about Scripture, but by the later elementary school years and certainly during the teen years, children begin to contemplate and ponder many of the deeper issues of life. If Scripture is readily available in their minds, it will strongly influence their thinking.

It will help us do God's will. "To do your will, O my God, is my desire; your law is within my heart" (Psalm 40:8). As the Lord commanded Joshua, "Do not let this Book of the Law depart from your mouth; meditate on it day and night, so that you may be careful to do everything written in it. Then you will be prosperous and successful" (Joshua 1:8).

God wants us to follow his perfect plan. He has chosen to reveal himself and his plans for us in his word. Part of knowing and doing God's will is to know and apply his word. If we and our children know the Bible and have it memorized and always available, we will be able to determine God's will at any given moment.

Memorized Scripture deeply affects other areas of life. It will protect your children's thought lives, give them ready words as they share Christ with friends, help them in later years if they counsel other Christians, and certainly give them confidence in the power and authority of the Bible to affect and control their lives.

Every committed Christian parent seeks God's best for their children. That may not mean fame and success, but it will mean a life dedicated to God and to doing his will. To get children started in that direction may be as simple as initiating a program of Scripture memory during your family devotional period.

I visited a family a few years ago who put a strong emphasis on Scripture memorization. One evening during the time I was there, they decided to have a contest. Each person present had to give a verse from each book of the Bible, starting with Genesis. When they could no longer quote a verse from a particular book, they had to drop out. Minor prophets were excluded. I am sorry to report that I dropped out early. I strained to remember a verse from Judges, but failed.

Their twelve-year-old son left the contest at Esther, the ten-year-old girl at Song of Solomon, and Mother and Dad carried through to Revelation.

Most Christian families would find it difficult to offer any competition at all to my friends. And, of course, little feats such as they performed are not the purpose of Scripture memory, but it proved that memory is not an impossible task. Careful training through the years builds a treasure store of memorized verses and passages.

Many individuals in the Bible demonstrated the value of memorized Scripture. Jesus used and quoted the Bible on many occasions. He overcame Satan's temptations by quoting Scripture, he corrected the erroneous thinking of the legalistic Pharisees by reminding them of the Scripture's teaching, and he often instructed his disciples by clearly explaining God's word to them.

The apostle Peter, when developing his preaching style, used direct quotes and long reviews of Israel's history. The apostle Paul, in shepherding and teaching the developing first-century church, often quoted the law to strengthen his teaching (see Galatians 3; Ephesians 4:7; and 1 Timothy 5:18).

The most powerful sermons we hear are sprinkled liberally with Bible quotations and references. The ideas of people lack strength and purpose, but the thoughts of Scripture give the message power and influence.

Hebrew boys were taught the law of God, called the Torah (the first five books of our Old Testament), as the basis of their education and as preparation for a life of service to God. They devoted much of their study time to memorizing the Torah.

> It would seem that this kind of education began as soon as the child could speak, and one may perhaps describe the nature of the instruction as the culture of memory. The place of the development of memory in the educational system of Israel is of primary importance. The purpose of the instruction was that the children may grow up to know and remember, and consequently obey, the law.[1]

While memorizing Scripture will help our children in their everyday lives, it also prepares them for the difficulties they will face as adults. Verses memorized in childhood have a way of returning in opportune moments to remind adults of specific truths of Scripture.

> Recounting his experiences as a prisoner of war, Captain Howard E. Rutledge writes: "How I struggled to recall those Scriptures

> and hymns! I had spent my first eighteen years in a Southern Baptist Sunday school, and I was amazed at how much I could recall; regrettably, I had not seen then the importance of memorizing verses from the Bible or learning gospel songs. Now, when I needed them, it was too late. I never dreamed that I would spend almost seven years (five of them in solitary confinement) in a prison in North Vietnam or that thinking about one memorized verse could have made a whole day bearable . . . How often I wished I had really worked to hide God's Word in my heart."[2]

Parents can realize the vital need for memorized Scripture in their children's lives if they can just imagine situations in that child's adult life in which memorized Scripture will be the only Bible available to them. In that way, the vision for teaching children to memorize the Bible will give impetus to the regular practice of memorization. But some will ask,

- Isn't it hard to memorize?
- Isn't it terribly time-consuming?
- Won't children be bored with it?
- Won't they forget most of the verses they learn?
- How can I expect my kids to memorize since I've never been able to do it?
- Why bother at home when they get plenty of memory verses in Sunday school?

Yes, it is occasionally hard, time-consuming, and possibly boring. And we do forget some of what we learn. But parents who truly want their children to know God's word will discover ways to overcome the obstacles in these questions because they know the lifelong value of memorizing Scripture.

Perhaps Scripture memory is ignored as part of the Christian life because, like its companion exercise, prayer, it takes work, discipline, and time. In our hasty, frenetic American culture, we rarely devote time to the contemplative aspects of our Christian lives. Rather we become busy with activities that, while fine in themselves, do little or nothing to develop spiritual depth.

When we approach the valuable things in life, we will always find obstacles. In something as important as Scripture memory, ignore the obstacles and press ahead. Find methods of helping your children memorize and retain Scripture. Use reward systems you design yourself. Always offer much praise and encouragement. And note the profits that accrue to your own spiritual welfare as you memorize with your children.

Here are a few suggestions that may help you carry on a successful program of Scripture memory with your family.

1. *Start slowly and simply.* If you suddenly decide to memorize five verses a week, the entire family will rebel. You will find it much better to learn one short verse each week and learn it well, than to learn several poorly and then quickly forget them.

Even if you memorize only one verse thoroughly each month, your family will know twelve verses well at the end of the year. And that is much better than partially knowing many verses, or not knowing any at all.

You can follow a plan such as Bible Memory Association's plan or The Navigators' Topical Memory System. However, you can also devise your own.

If your children are young, select short verses such as the following. Allow them to experience some success before attempting more ambitious goals.

- Psalm 23:1: The Lord is my Shepherd, I shall lack nothing.
- Matthew 5:8: Blessed are the pure in heart, for they will see God.
- Romans 3:23: For all have sinned and fall short of the glory of God.
- Ephesians 6:1: Children, obey your parents in the Lord, for this is right.
- Philippians 4:4: Rejoice in the Lord always. I will say it again: Rejoice.
- 1 Thessalonians 5:16: Be joyful always.
- 1 Peter 5:7: Cast all your anxiety on him because he cares for you.

You might want to choose parts of verses when you are beginning to memorize. The chapter and verse divisions in Scripture were not inspired, and you do no disservice to the Bible to learn only part of a verse. If you want to learn a long verse, take as much as two or three weeks to learn it well.

Later, when you have firmly established patterns and practices for successful Scripture memory, you can learn two or three verses a week if you like. However, always cut back if you find that your children are not retaining what they have learned, or if they seem bogged down and frustrated with the pace you are trying to set.

2. *Follow a simple learning process.* Begin by saying the reference over several times. Then look up the verse in the Bible and read it. Then say the reference again a few times. Add the first phrase or the first several words of the verse. Always say the reference before beginning the verse. Many adult Christians know quite a few Bible verses from their Sunday school days, but when asked where the verses are located can only say, "Well, I know it's in the Bible somewhere."

Always learn small portions of the verse correctly before moving on. Say the verse out loud together as a family and then have individual family members say it.

This process will take only one or two minutes of your devotional time. Each time you have family devotions, repeat what you have already learned and add the next phrase, until the verse is well learned. Review the verse for several days, either by saying it in unison or asking one family member to say it, until you are certain each person knows it well.

3. *Review, repeat, reinforce.* Even the most retentive memory cannot hold material without occasional review. Plan to bring out verses for review often enough so that the initial learning was not wasted effort. If you learn a verse during the first week of the month, review it two days each week until the end of the month—and occasionally after that—and you will find that it remains firmly fixed in the minds of your children.

Perhaps once every two or three months devote your entire devotional period to a verse contest. Divide the family into two groups and hold a "verse bee" patterned after the spelling bee. The competition will show you if your children are retaining the verses they have memorized. Perhaps you can increase the number of verses your family memorizes, or you may find that you must allow more time for review.

Use any other methods you can create to reinforce the verses you are learning. If your children can read, type or print the verse on small cards (recipe size works well) and tape the cards to the bathroom mirrors, your children's dresser mirrors, or drop them in their school lunch bags. Repeat the verse from time to time in situations other than devotions, perhaps just before bedtime or as you ride in the car. Offer small and unexpected rewards occasionally for a perfectly quoted verse.

The impact and power of God's word in the lives of your children will reward every effort you make in helping them memorize the Bible. Don't allow the Sunday school program, the Bible club program, or the Christian school's requirements to rob you of the great privilege of leading your children in a simple, consistent, progressive Scripture memory plan in your own home. You will benefit as much as they do.

Notes

1. *The Zondervan Pictorial Encyclopedia of the Bible*, ed. Merrill C. Tenney (Grand Rapids, Michigan: Zondervan Publishing House, 1975), Volume 2, page 213.
2. G. Roger Schoenhals, "Tuck Away a Verse a Day," *Christian Life* 36:9 (January, 1975), page 18.

Suggested Resources

Topical Memory System. Colorado Springs, Colorado: NavPress, 1969.

5 *Music*

A SHORT TIME ago, I visited a friend with a two-year-old daughter. As we sat talking, the little girl played with some toys in the same room. Gradually I realized that she was singing, and I paused for a moment in the conversation to listen. From that tiny, curly-haired girl with a little voice came the words of the magnificent hymn, "Holy, Holy, Holy."

I exclaimed to my friend that her little girl seemed very young to be singing such a powerful hymn.

"She will sing anything I teach her," her mother said. "Sometimes I run out of ideas and just sing what we sang in church the Sunday before. She always picks it right up."

That little girl probably has more musical potential than most children, but all children respond to music. Singing together as a family offers a fine opportunity for worship and teaching and praise. Every Christian family should experience the pleasure of singing together. The devotional time should serve as a focal point for teaching songs and singing together, and can be a prelude for extended times of song—in the car, at the table, on vacations, and while working together.

Perhaps you feel your family lacks talent in the area of music. Musical ability, whether minimal or extensive, doesn't affect enjoyment or personal participation. Our family enjoys music, and each member of the family sings or plays an instrument or does both. But even if we did not have some musical background, we would still include music as part of our spiritual experience.

Martin Luther understood the importance of music in the life of a Christian when he said, "Music is the art of the prophets, the only art that calms the agitations of the soul; it is one of the most magnificent and delightful presents God has given us."[1] He must have felt something of that "magnificent and delightful present" when he composed the incomparable "A Mighty Fortress Is Our God."

A mighty fortress is our God,
A bulwark never failing;
Our helper He amid the flood
of mortal ills prevailing.
For still our ancient foe
doth seek to work us woe—
His craft and power are great,
And armed with cruel hate,
On earth is not His equal.

The Bible records the stories of many people who sang, and relates the reasons for writing their songs. Usually, they burst into song, or composed songs in a mood of joy and response to their love of God or appreciation for what he had done for them. Here are a few examples:

- Moses and all the people of Israel sang a song of praise after God had safely delivered them from the pursuing Egyptians (see Exodus 15:1-19).
- Deborah, a judge in Israel, and Barak, the leader of Israel's fighting forces, sang of a marvelous victory over their enemies (see Judges 5:1-31).
- David composed and sang a song of deliverance after he had been saved from King Saul's vengeful pursuit (see 2 Samuel 22:1-51).
- The nation of Israel sang a song of gratitude after God had provided water for them in the barren desert (see Numbers 21:17-18).

- The Levites formed a choir which performed for all Israel, along with orchestral accompaniment, to celebrate the purification of the temple and the offering of ritual sacrifices (see 2 Chronicles 29:27-28).
- The disciples and Jesus ended the first communion service with a hymn (see Matthew 26:30).
- Paul and Silas sang hymns in jail at midnight. The Scripture records that other prisoners were awake and listening (see Acts 16:25).
- The book of Hebrews records a quote from Psalms regarding Jesus who said, "I will declare your name to my brothers; in the presence of the congregation I will sing your praises" (Hebrews 2:12).
- The Bible records even ships, woods, and trees singing, so perhaps in some way unknown to us, all of nature sings to the glory of God.

God intends that singing be an integral part of our Christian experience. Singing during family devotions impresses on our children the purposes God has for music in our lives. Several of the reasons for singing are mentioned in Scripture.

To express our joy to the Lord. "Come, let us sing for joy to the Lord; let us shout aloud to the Rock of our salvation. Let us come before him with thanksgiving and extol him with music and song" (Psalm 95:1-2). "Shout for joy to the Lord, all the earth. Serve the Lord with gladness; come before him with joyful songs" (Psalm 100:1-2).

Most Christians associate happiness with singing. Although sad sentiments can be expressed through music, most people sing when they feel pleased, secure, and joyous about life. We can observe this characteristic in our children. They rarely sing when unhappy or angry or displeased. But when they are contented and satisfied, they often begin unconsciously singing or whistling or humming portions of songs while they play or work.

When they are sad, they may like to listen to music—often a way of escape into another world. Then the music is often in a minor key and is morbidly introspective. Some of the music in the secular world is destructive and immoral. Replace this with good music.

Parents can influence this part of their children's Christian experience by insuring that when they sing, it will be with words of praise and joy, rather than repetitious television ditties or foolish and misleading sentimental songs. Songs taught early and repeated frequently will remain with our children for life.

It seems to be in the nature of children to sing. They might repeat musical commercials, songs from children's television programs, or Christian melodies learned from us, from records, or from tape recordings.

How pleasant it is to hear children expressing their joy and happiness by singing the words of a Christian hymn or song.

To offer praise and worship. A veteran missionary to China, Isobel Kuhn, tells of an instance of spontaneous praise in song. A group of missionaries were living in a mission guest home. Two of their colleagues had been prisoners in Communist China for several years. On the morning they heard of the release of the prisoners, the missionaries spontaneously burst into a jubilant rendition of the hymn of praise known as "The Doxology."[2]

Praise God from whom all blessings flow,
Praise Him all creatures here below.
Praise Him above, ye heavenly host,
Praise Father, Son, and Holy Ghost.

Small children may not be specifically aware that they sing to praise God, but they will develop an appreciation for the part music plays in worshiping God. And as they sing the same truths again and again, those ideas will become an integral part of their spiritual thinking. We can prepare young children for the experience of singing praise and worship by teaching them appropriate songs.

The Psalms tell us of the songs David used in praise.

Psalm 40:3: He put a new song in my mouth, a hymn of praise to our God.

Psalm 66:1-2: Shout with joy to God, all the earth! Sing to the glory of his name; offer him glory and praise!

Psalm 69:30: I will praise God's name in song and glorify him with thanksgiving.

Many times praise flows more easily through music than through spoken words. Children, along with their parents, can learn to praise and worship God through songs that honor him and his word.

A children's song composed of just two phrases offers a simple but effective method of praise:

Praise him, praise him, all ye little children;
God is love, God is love!
Praise him, praise him, all ye little children;
God is love, God is love!

How simple yet how profound!

Another song that children have sung for years repeats two phrases over and over:

Hallelu, hallelu, hallelu, hallelujah,
Praise ye the Lord.
Hallelu, hallelu, hallelu, hallelujah,
Praise ye the Lord.
Praise ye the Lord, hallelujah,
Praise ye the Lord, hallelujah,
Praise ye the Lord, hallelujah,
Praise ye the Lord.

Many songs offer words with more specific themes of praise and worship:

- "Thank You, Lord"
- "Hallelujah, What a Savior"
- "Praise Ye the Father"

Some of the concepts in the songs we teach our children surpass their immediate understanding. But they will have memorized the words and melodies. Their understanding of the concepts will develop in time.

To teach truth. Music figured strongly in the life of the early Christian church. They no doubt used the songs and psalms written by King David and King Solomon as well as some of their own compositions.

Spiritual awakenings seem to be accompanied by an upsurge in musical composition by men and women who revere and love God and are eager to promote his truth through music.

The nation of Israel peaked spiritually during the reigns of David and Solomon, both of whom wrote copiously of the truths of God. 1 Kings 4:32 records that Solomon wrote 1005 songs.

During the Protestant Reformation of the sixteenth century, Martin Luther (and others) wrote many inspiring and refreshing hymns which reinforced the renewed emphasis on biblical truth in that time.

Then as the Reformation gathered momentum and matured, other composers appeared who furthered the teachings of the Bible by setting large portions of Scripture to music. Bach, Handel, and Beethoven wrote in the sixteenth and seventeenth centuries.

In the eighteenth century, as John Wesley led his followers to form the Methodist movement, his brother Charles gave heart to the work by presenting the budding church with numerous hymns, many of which are still familiar in our hymnbooks today:

- "Jesus, Lover of My Soul"
- "Hark the Herald Angels Sing"
- "Christ the Lord Is Risen Today"
- "O For a Thousand Tongues to Sing"

The spiritual revivals of the nineteenth and early twentieth centuries produced such hymn writers as Fanny Crosby and Phillip Bliss.

The introduction of Sunday school two hundred years ago

prompted the writing of more simple songs for children.

Today we live in a time of prolific music production in the Christian community. Some of the songs lack spiritual substance, tending rather to promote emotional experience, but much of the composition is God-honoring and uplifting. Scripture set to contemporary rhythms has wide appeal for children and young people. Many truly gifted composers are writing and arranging biblical stories and teachings in clever and appealing ways that enhance the desire of our children to sing the truths of God.

Consider exposing your family to such children's cantatas as:

- "It's Cool in the Furnace"
- "100% Chance of Rain"
- "Nathaniel the Grublet"

Are you looking for a spiritual freshness in your family devotions, a unique way to implant spiritual teaching in the minds of your children? Introduce music and repeat it until it grips their memories and understanding.

To thank God. "Speak to one another with psalms, hymns and spiritual songs. Sing and make music in your heart to the Lord, always giving thanks to God the Father for everything, in the name of our Lord Jesus Christ" (Ephesians 5:19-20).

1 Chronicles 16:7-36 records the song of thanks that David composed in appreciation for the installation of the ark of God in the city of Jerusalem. In addition to the beautiful song of thanks, musically gifted Levites received special appointments to provide instrumental music of thanks, using lyres, harps, cymbals, and trumpets. Evidently the sound of this music would bring to the minds of the Israelites the goodness of the Lord and stimulate their thanks to him.

Sometimes we find difficulty in adequately expressing our thanks and appreciation to God for his general goodness to all of Christendom or his specific kindness to us as individuals. We can allow hymns and songs to represent our feelings of gratitude. We can lead our children in thanking God for his love and kindness.

In your own family, during the devotional time, or spontaneously at any time, music provides a vehicle for expressing joy, praise, worship, truth, and thanks. Use such simple songs as "Thank You, Lord, for Saving My Soul" or "Thank You, Jesus."

In many practical ways we can incorporate music into our spiritual experience.

1. Sing when your children are young, before they develop a reserve about singing aloud. Allow singing to become a natural part of your family experience.

   One of our children did enter a period in the teens when audible singing proved a painful experience even within the family circle, so we did not insist on participation. Eventually, although it took a couple of years, that child once again started singing aloud.
2. Use short simple songs for young children. Songs with repetitive phrases work well. Young children's memories absorb lyrics and music incredibly fast. Notice how they learn a Sunday school song in one session.
3. Action songs appeal to small children and pre-adolescents.
4. Invest in a children's songbook (see the bibliography) to give you ideas for new songs.
5. Use any instruments that family members play—the piano, guitar, band instruments, stringed instruments, or harmonica. Encourage your children to prepare occasional musical "specials" for the enjoyment and appreciation of the rest of the family.
6. Use taped or recorded music to learn new songs. Occasionally use such music for listening only, but on the whole, children benefit more from participating than listening. Borrow tapes and records from friends and your church library to cut costs.
7. Use an entire devotional time to sing. Begin with a portion of Scripture set to music, learn a new song, and continue with a prayer set to music ("For God So Loved the World" or "Thank You, Lord"). Perhaps one confident family member could sing a solo or two.
8. When you teach a new song, sing it again and again—twice a

day for one week—until it becomes ingrained in the minds of your children. When you hear your children singing or humming the song around your home, you will know it has taken hold.

9. Ask your children's Sunday school teacher what they are singing during the Sunday school hour. Sing those songs at home to reinforce what the children learn at church.
10. Sing thanks to God. Many occasions give opportunity for thanks.

- Grandma has recovered from a serious illness.
- You have just completed a fun family vacation.
- Dad received a promotion.
- Mom is serving steak for dinner.
- Your lost dog has been found.
- Sister received a high mark on an algebra test.

Detail the event for your children and sing together,

Jesus, we just want to thank you,
Jesus, we just want to thank you,
Jesus, we just want to thank you
Thank you for being so good.

11. As your children grow older, sing together the stately hymns of the Christian faith:

- "To God Be the Glory" by Fanny J. Crosby
- "How Great Thou Art" by Carl Boberg
- "Holy, Holy, Holy" by Reginald Heber
- "Come, Thou Almighty King" (source unknown)
- "Great Is Thy Faithfulness" by Thomas O. Chisholm

Younger children may not fully understand the doctrine behind these marvelous hymns, but they can learn to appreciate them before they fully understand. Check your church library to find a book giving the background and circumstances under which some of these hymns were written. For example: *Crusader Hymns and Hymn Stories.*

12. Many passages of Scripture and Bible stories have been set to contemporary as well as traditional melodies. Teach your children these songs, for they serve a double purpose. They give musical enjoyment while reinforcing the word of God in their lives.

We made it a practice to require each child to be involved in some kind of music—playing an instrument, or singing in the choir—each year until they graduated from high school. You may be thinking, *I can't carry a tune in a bushel basket, so how can I teach my children?* We could say, "Make a joyful noise unto the Lord." Music is such a part of the church and the Christian life—expressing what the soul feels—that we need to help our children develop it in their lives even when we are not very proficient. Often, one family member shines in music. Use that ability to help the others. You will never regret introducing them to music that reflects the life in Christ.

Notes

1. *The International Encyclopedia of Quotations* (Chicago: J. G. Ferguson Publishing Company, 1969), page 506.
2. Isobel Kuhn, *Green Leaves in Drought Times* (Chicago: Moody Press, 1957), page 11.

Suggested Resources

Billy Graham Team, ed. *Crusader Hymns and Hymn Stories.* Chicago: Hope Publishing Co., 1966, 1967.

Hymns for the Family of God. Nashville, Tennessee: Paragon Associates, Inc., 1976.

Lively Choruses, Vols. 1, 2, and 3. Singspiration. Grand Rapids, Michigan: Zondervan Music Corporation, 1957.

6 Combining the Secular and the Sacred

WHEN OUR CHILDREN were in elementary school, I detected that they lacked confidence during certain social situations. So for several weeks we followed our Bible reading and prayer time with a course in etiquette.

We began with introductions—how to introduce a child to an adult, a woman to a man, an adult to a child. We used a role-playing method. Our youngest child would play "Grandma." She was four years old at the time. The other children would assume the role of introducer or introducee.

We moved on to table manners, including table conversation. We talked about making others feel at ease. I shared with the children that etiquette is simply a collection of ideas and guidelines for us to help other people feel comfortable in our presence.

After a few weeks of our quick course in good manners, we all went to dinner together to practice our newfound skills.

During the learning sessions, our children laughed and joked as they practiced introductions, flipped the dinner napkins to their laps with a flourish, or rushed to open the car door for one another. But we noticed that when the real situations arose, they responded with ease.

Since that time, they have exhibited some sad lapses in etiquette. In fact, a few years after the home training, some close friends of ours told us that one of our children seemed discourteous and sullen when the family came to our home. We had noticed it too, but in the way of all parents, hoped that others had not.

We appreciated the honesty of our friends in bringing the child's need to our attention, but we felt that the child by nature was not uncivil, merely shy and uncomfortable with anyone other than peers. However, in life we must all relate to a wide variety of people, not a narrow group of our own choosing.

We talked about how we could help the child. Rather than using direct confrontation, we decided to involve the entire family in another series of role-playing situations designed to give confidence with a wide range of people.

We discussed and practiced how to—

- stand when an adult enters a room;
- always look another person in the eyes when speaking;
- offer a hand as a gesture of friendship and welcome;
- be prepared with "small talk" to cover any early awkwardness when meeting someone;
- invite visitors to be seated;
- be prepared to donate a few minutes of personal time to making visitors comfortable;
- offer something to drink. Even seven- and eight-year-old children can make and serve refreshments.

Although these suggestions were hard for the child to practice, we began to see slow improvement. Today that child seems quite secure in meeting new people and adapting to social situations.

Over a period of years, we have determined several reasons for adding similar "extras" to our family devotional times.

We can help our children relate their spiritual views to the world at large. We want our children to identify their spiritual training with all areas of life. The truths of Scripture are not to be isolated from real life. Rather, biblical truth relates practically to our everyday circumstances. Spiritual truth and everyday living should be interwoven and interdependent.

When we begin a project, we try to help our children understand how it relates to the truth of God's word. Making that correlation is simple if the project concerns missions or giving. But even when the activity seems secular in nature, some relationship to spiritual teaching should be evident.

When we discuss politics, community affairs, and world geography, we can help our children see the hand of God in all aspects of life. If we play a rousing game of kickball, we can comment on the healthy bodies God has given us.

If we frequently apply scriptural principles to our extra activities, our children will see God's pattern of involvement and influence in all of our daily experiences. We won't need to mention it every time we present an activity. God wants us to enjoy life, every aspect of life.

We don't feel compelled to make a spiritual application for every activity. Some projects merely entertain. We use them to bring an element of fun and joy to our times together as a family.

We always finish our devotional time with the additional activities. That way, if we do run short of time, prayer and Scripture have come first.

We, not the world, will teach our children. Our children receive so much influence and teaching from sources other than home or church. Many of the values and concepts they hear at school, from playmates, or on television run counter to the life values we are trying to instill in them. We cannot control every input into their lives. But we can influence them at home.

One way to exert control over the negative inputs and pressures our children experience is to select special topics and subjects for study and discussion. Then present them so attractively that the children enjoy them and want more. We can choose activities according to the needs of our children, or use special activities to correct instruction they receive elsewhere that may not meet the standards we have for them.

Children hear a great deal of wrong information regarding moral issues. They hear of abortion, homosexuality, casual sex, birth control, and situational ethics. We can help them formulate their opinions and values based on scriptural truth. They need our guidance to learn how to view these issues from a biblical perspective. When children reach adolescence—perhaps as early as pre-adolescence—these topics should be discussed openly and often. They should always be discussed in the light of God's word.

In our family we plan to read and talk about portions of *Whatever Happened to the Human Race?* by Francis A. Schaeffer and C. Everett Koop, M.D. We feel it will give our children a healthy perspective for considering God's value of a human life. It will open areas for discussion that might not otherwise come up in our conversations.

Some of the negative influences draw our children away from God very subtly. We scarcely recognize what happens in their lives until a large problem looms. If we consistently watch for such problems and—even more important—if we offer opportunities to discuss those problems, we have a chance to change and redirect our children's thinking.

We have three daughters in our family, and like women everywhere, they are interested in clothes and fashion. When Jerry was traveling for a few weeks, and our son was attending camp, we took a short course in fashion. We talked about matching colors, fabrics, and patterns. We cut wish wardrobes from magazines and modeled the ideal costume for one another.

Throughout the project I brought up the need for modesty in our dress. We don't want our girls to be puritanical, but we do emphasize that they represent Jesus Christ, and for his sake they need to be attractive and pleasant. We talked, too, of the beauty that comes from within and the need to be a lovely person in character as well as appearance.

Many projects will fascinate your children to the point that they will want to continue at times other than devotions. We want to see that interest develop, for it indicates the positive influence we can have with them.

We can contribute to our children's intellectual development. When our son was small, I noticed he was sometimes restless and distracted when I read Bible stories to him. Visual aids helped, but he seemed to want more participation. Remembering that my youngest sister used to join in family devotions before she started school by reading part of the passage from the King James Bible, I decided to teach Steve to read. He was three years old.

He quickly passed beyond his first little reading book about Jesus to more advanced reading. His interest in devotions increased when he could participate by reading a part of the story.

Being young and inexperienced parents, we assumed all of our children would be reading and participating in devotions when they were three or four years old. That was a poor assumption! Our children quickly educated us. What appeals to one child may be distasteful to another. One of our children did not begin to enjoy reading until she was twelve years old!

We can supplement our children's intellectual development by choosing activities that will stimulate and enlarge their thinking. Just a simple thing such as asking them a question starts the thinking process and keeps their brains active.

Recently Jerry presented a project to our children. He challenged them to use a world atlas and find a country of their choice. Then they returned to the next family devotional time to tell Jerry and me the name of the country. If we could not name a neighboring country, they would receive a small monetary prize.

They spent much time poring over the atlas. Jerry and I felt fairly confident of keeping our money because Jerry has traveled quite widely and I have always been interested in geography. We did, by guessing, name a country bordering Yemen. But they stumped us on Corsica. We were close, but not close enough. Chalk one up for the children, but one for Jerry, too, for he challenged them to think, research, and strategize.

Children will occupy their minds with something. Parents can direct the thinking of their children by offering plans and activities that will cause their minds to work and develop in a positive way.

We can direct our children's social and cultural development. By exposing our children to a variety of situations and experiences, we can stimulate their social and cultural development. Most children naturally acquire some finesse in interpersonal relationships. Such development is forced on them through family interactions and classroom situations. However, we can provide specific help through training.

Simple etiquette exercises such as the ones our family tried will help a child gain confidence in the situations he encounters every day. You can choose more advanced activities to help children foster and maintain deeper friendships, learn to extend themselves to others with needs, and even, as they mature, to counsel others.

Our family practiced a technique around the dinner table that we hoped would give all of us an awareness of each other's needs. We did not ask for anything to be passed, but rather we waited for someone to notice that we needed something.

A small thing? Yes, but we found our children far more alert to the needs of other family members and we heard such things as, "Would you care for more spinach?" "Did the salt and pepper reach you?" "Butter for you?"

We continued this procedure even with guests present, although we didn't ask them to participate. If we were following the procedure properly, they didn't even notice what was going on. After two weeks we trusted that some sensitivity developed that would carry on beyond the planned activity.

Culturally, parents can expand their children's views and appreciation of art, music, literature, and science. In the broadest sense, culture refers to all of human progress and achievement.

If you listen to a record together, or read your children a biography of Thomas Edison, or give them clay and ask them to shape an animal, you are giving them cultural enrichment in a small sense.

We can help our children develop an understanding and enjoyment of the fine things our culture has given us. At the same time we can discuss some of the trends our culture is following, such as materialism and immorality, that counter the values we see in Scripture.

We can enhance family communication. Every conscientious parent in our fast-paced society experiences frustration in trying to maintain family unity. We have found that extra activities during our devotional times help in drawing our interests and thinking together as a family. Jerry and I were surprised and dismayed when we realized how quickly our children grew and became involved in outside activities—sports, music, church groups—all commendable, but all drawing our children away from the family circle. We found that by varying our special activities we could focus together on things of interest.

Sometimes that meant that we must do together what one child was committed to doing. We might all attend Kathy's gymnastics meet. Then, instead of formal devotions, we would have a time of prayer or praise on the drive home. Or we would attend Karen's choir concert, and then at home make popcorn and read a Scripture portion together.

Even though we are sometimes unable to conduct devotions in a structured way, we refuse to allow them to be crowded out entirely. We use the moments we can to share together with our children.

When we do have extended times together at home, we often focus on things that will give our children a sense of family and heritage. We read letters from grandparents, cousins, aunts and uncles. We look at family pictures together. We place a phone call to a family member who isn't at home with us. We include whatever activities we feel will strengthen our immediate and extended family ties.

As you plan to include extra activities, keep in mind that—

1. Scripture and prayer must always predominate in the devotional time.
2. Secular activities can be included regularly or occasionally.
3. Extras are more appealing and effective with children of elementary school age and older. Younger children lack the attention span to go much beyond Bible teaching and prayer.

Now for some specific suggestions. These ideas are sketchy and should be used just to stimulate your thinking about activities that would bring enjoyment to your particular family. Here are possible topics or areas of interest.

Social Concern

Would you like your children to develop an awareness of their fortunate circumstances as compared with people who live in other parts of the world? Use your imagination to determine ways to help them understand their privileged position and, in concern, reach out to help others.

1. After devotions, have each child go to his room and pick out several items of clothing he no longer needs or wears, and one he especially likes, and gather them together for a church or organizational clothing drive. Help your children learn to give to someone what is meaningful to them, not just discards.

2. Eat rice and bread for one meal a week and give the money normally spent on food to an organization that cares for needy people in other parts of the world. Our family followed this practice for over two years and the devotions we held around those dinners were especially meaningful. We kept a small bank at the table, then deposited the money in the bank after each rice dinner to visually aid our children in understanding their contribution. When we received a letter from the organization we donated to, we would read the letter together.

3. If you know of a food drive or collection, tell your children about it. Then go to your pantry or cupboard and allow each child to pick items to give. Encourage them to give the best—pie cherries, not string beans; walnuts, not oatmeal; chocolate chips, not powdered milk. Children can learn to be concerned for the preferences and needs of others.

Nature

1. Take five minutes after devotions to go outdoors and collect as many varieties of leaves as you can find. Notice their colors and varied shapes. Talk about God's creativity. Press the leaves between two pieces of waxed paper with a warm iron and use for the next day's place mats.

2. In the summertime observe the stars. Identify some of the constellations for your children. (Use your encyclopedia.) Talk about the stars, their distances from earth, their brilliance, their size.

3. Bring a bowl of water to the table. Ask your children to name the places they see water (ocean, lake, bathtub, water glass, fish tank, rivers). Then talk about the need for water in our daily lives.

Good Literature

1. Your local library will be a great help. Spend half an hour looking through books suitable for your children. Talk to the librarian. Gather suggestions for books from friends. Then spend a week reading a good book to your children. Always stop reading in an exciting place so your children will be eager for you to resume.

2. Read a children's version of Bunyan's *Pilgrim's Progress.*

3. As a major project, read through C.S. Lewis' *Chronicles of Narnia.* Our family has read through this beautiful series at least twice and we are beginning once again. Lewis' fine literary style and fascinating stories never become tiresome.

4. Include poetry from time to time, perhaps something by Robert Frost or Rudyard Kipling.

5. Do you enjoy humor? Our family had many a good chuckle as we read through *Cheaper by the Dozen* and *Belles on their Toes* by Frank Galbraith, or occasional humorous articles from the *Reader's Digest.* Ask each child to bring one good joke to share at the beginning or end of family devotions.

6. Read a play together with each family member taking a different part.

7. Consider reading through some children's classics like *Robinson Crusoe, The Black Stallion* series, *The Five Little Peppers,* or *Heidi.*

Family

Many American families are separated because of the rapidly changing employment circumstances we have in our country. If such is your case, devise ways to emphasize your family background and the relatives your children don't see on a regular basis. Give your children a sense of the heritage they have through their families.

1. Read appropriate portions from letters that arrive from grandparents and other family members.

2. Bring out pictures of various family members and tell a story or two about them, or some interesting feature about their lives.

3. Show your children pictures of yourselves as children and relate to them one especially happy incident you can recall from your childhood.

4. If relatives who are Christians are visiting with you, have them give their testimonies.

5. Pass around paper and pencils and encourage your children to write a short note to their grandparents.

Politics and Government

Any child who has reached school age should understand something of the government of our land and the political system. Make your explanations in simple terms. Even our government leaders have trouble understanding all of the complexities of our system! As Christian parents we can give our children the right attitude toward our government and teach them responsible conduct as Christian citizens.

1. On the day you vote, clip a sample ballot from the newspaper. Show it to your children and explain a few of the issues. Describe a few of the candidates.

2. Borrow a book from the library or use your encyclopedia to show your children the Declaration of Independence. Do the same with the Constitution of the United States.

3. Ask your children to list all the laws they have to obey daily. Explain that such laws provide protection and community benefits. A few would be to:

- obey speed limits.
- pay sales taxes.
- keep the dog leashed.
- attend school.

4. Show your children pictures of the White House and

other buildings in Washington, D.C. Explain the importance and use of each one.

5. As they get older, involve your children in political discussions on issues or elections that are current.

6. Relate political issues to Scripture whenever possible. Help your children become tolerant of opposing views.

Music

Although chapter 5 details the use of spiritually oriented music during the devotional time, you can increase your child's appreciation for other music as well. A record player or a piano or guitar are helpful, but not necessary.

1. If one of your children is studying a musical instrument, ask him to prepare a special piece to play for the family. Set a tone of approval and appreciation for his efforts. Don't allow your other children to ridicule any squeeks, squawks, or sour notes!

2. Play a symphonic piece on the record player (you can check them out from your library) and ask your children to identify various instruments.

3. If your family doesn't care for symphonic music, do the same thing with good country hoedown music.

4. Teach your children a song that was special to you when you were young.

5. Sing in rounds. Start with "Row, Row, Row Your Boat" and move on to more complicated songs.

6. If you have children in their teens and they are beginning to show an interest in popular or rock music, have them play a record for you and then together discuss the lyrics. Allow them to explain what they feel the song says, then encourage them to compare that philosophy with God's standards. Keep the conversation friendly. Listen, don't criticize.

Finances

Children need to learn early in life the value of money, its source, its importance, and its use. They must understand that Dad's wallet and Mother's purse don't contain an endless supply. We can help them achieve success in the use of their money by giving them counsel and guidance.

1. Give each child a piece of paper and help them draw up a budget based on their income, whether that comes from an allowance or a job. Stress giving and saving first, then spending. Encourage consistent record keeping and check the budgets again in two weeks.

2. If you have teenagers in your home, have them read portions or all of *You can Be Financially Free* by George Fooshee. Be sure to cover the material on the cost of automobiles.

3. Establish a giving project, perhaps a missionary or a special fund drive at your church, or a family with particular needs. Suggest that each child decide privately how much he can give. Once a week for a month have him bring that money to the devotional time. No one needs to know what others give, but all will be eager to see the total at the end of the month.

Sports and Games

Children always respond with pleasure when you conclude the devotional time by saying, "Okay, kids, we have just enough time for three good hands of PIT." Our children enjoy a competitive encounter and we try to include a game of some kind frequently. Remember to vary the types and intensities of the games to give each child a chance to excel in one particular activity.

Insist on good sportsmanship and mutual encouragement. Always stop the game immediately if you hear criticism, complaining, or bickering. Merely say, "We started this game to have fun. Quarreling isn't fun. We'll try again another time."

1. Play a table game that is consistent with your children's ages and interests. Try PIT (rowdy but fun), backgammon, Monopoly, and Boggle.

2. Learn to juggle. Award a small prize to the one who first keeps three items in the air for fifteen seconds. I recommend tennis balls. Harder objects can cause damage either to household furniture or toes.

3. Spend five minutes playing frisbee, one frisbee per two people, and keep them flying.

4. Organize a "family book of records" and offer occasional contests to see who can get his or her name in the record book. Use activities such as the largest bubble blown from one piece of bubble gum, the greatest number of skips with a jump rope, the longest time balancing the narrow end of an umbrella on the palm of the hand, and so on.

5. Divide the family into teams. Play ten minutes of softball, organize a race, play touch football, have a tug of war. Use time limits rather than innings or quarters.

6. Give the sports minded in the family a chance to share their knowledge and excitement about football scores, individual player records, or the upcoming big game.

Animals

Most children love animals and are fascinated to learn more about them. Use various activities about animals that will appeal especially to children of elementary school age.

1. Gather pictures and information about contrasting animals, perhaps a mouse and an elephant. Talk about similarities and differences. Both are grey, but what a difference in size! Discuss the relationship of these animals to human beings.

2. Find some information about marsupials, animals with a pouch. Children feel a special attraction for the odd or the unusual. Talk about ways this animal takes care of its young.

3. Bring your dog or cat to the family group, or borrow your neighbor's dog if you don't have one of your own. Talk about reasons a family likes animals.

4. Has your child done a special study on animals for a school project? Let him present it to the family.

5. Always take advantage of a guest in your home who may know something special about animals, or have an animal story to tell. Our children always enjoy hearing my father describe his boyhood horseback-riding adventures, or the variety of personalities in the cows he has milked.

6. Have a contest to see who can name the most of a particular variety of animal, like animals with hoofs, animals that

live in the mountains, animals that live in the ground, and so on. Award a small prize to the winner.

These are some of the possibilities for including activities and information to teach and please your children. Allow the preceding ideas to stimulate your thinking toward areas of special interest to your own children. More topics?

- Health
- Sex education
- Missions
- Art
- History
- Bible geography
- Fashion
- Careers
- Travel
- Fishing
- Cars
- Space travel
- Other countries
- Photography

Your ideas and activities don't need to be elaborate, but they must be interesting and relevant. If your children lose interest, drop the topic. You achieve no benefit in plowing through an activity to the bitter end if no one enjoys it.

These activities should never be heavy or boring. Rather they should provide a spark, be a drawing card, a bonus for your children. These activities should always leave the children wanting more.

Suggested Resources

Games and Activities

Childcraft - the How and Why Library, Vol. 9. Chicago: Field Enterprises Educational Corp., 1964.

Dads Only Newsletter. Julian, California: Dads Only, P.O. Box 340, Julian, California.

Fluegelman, Andrew, ed. *The New Games Book*. Garden City, New York: Doubleday and Co., Inc., 1976.

Reading

Childcraft - the How and Why Library, Vols. 1 and 2. Chicago: Field Enterprises Educational Corp., 1964.

Lewis, C. S. *Chronicles of Narnia.* New York: The Macmillan Co., 1970.

Korfker, Dena. *Can You Tell Me?* Grand Rapids, Michigan: Zondervan Publishing House, 1970.

Palmer, Bernard. *Danny Orlis Series.* Chicago: Moody Press, 1979.

Wilder, Laura Ingalls. *Little House Books.* New York: Harper and Row, 1941.

7 Tots

TOTS PRESENT AN enchanting picture as they learn spiritual values and truths by singing of Jesus in their soprano voices, looking at Bible storybooks and praying in simple, direct terms. Parents need to focus not just on the sweetness of such scenes, but on the seriousness of establishing their preschool children in the basics of knowing, trusting, and loving God as their heavenly Father. Children of preschool age learn quickly and without seriously questioning their teachers. That attitude gives parents great opportunities as well as great responsibilities.

When our children were toddlers, we often concentrated our devotions on the life of Jesus. We wanted to introduce them to the Son of God who had come to reveal God to us and to assure our eternal life with him.

They enjoyed any illustrations that made the story more vivid. They especially liked any story regarding Jesus' travels on the Sea of Galilee, for then we all trooped to the bathroom where we would enact the story in a tub of water with small plastic boats and toy people.

How do these little ones learn? What processes do they go through to acquire knowledge? Can parents take advantage of those processes?

Children learn by observation. Before a baby accomplishes tasks for himself, he busies himself with watching. Before he can grasp anything, move under his own power, or express himself with a smile, he watches and learns by observing. He discovers his parents' faces hovering above him and he learns to distinguish faces displaying smiles or frowns. From the time he can focus his eyes, a child learns by watching.

Notice a little child's eyes. Watch him for ten minutes. He constantly focuses on the source of activity or interest in the room. He swivels his head, or his whole body if necessary, to determine where the action is and to see what is going on. He keeps up this attentiveness almost constantly while awake, along with squirming and stretching his muscles. Sometimes he concentrates so effectively and intensely that he completely wears himself out and falls asleep. He will watch others at the table with great awareness until he suddenly droops forward and dozes off with his head in his mashed potatoes. Or he rides in the car, observing the passing scene with such alertness that he suddenly rolls to the side of his car seat and in moments is asleep.

Christian parents need to be aware of the constant observation that occupies their preschoolers and take advantage of it in their spiritual training.

As they grow older, children learn by participation. First they observe, then they get involved with all their senses—taste, touch, and smell as well as sight. Personality has some effect on their degree of involvement, but preschoolers can't resist entering into any activity that intrigues them and welcomes them.

Recently, while helping in the church nursery, I saw this involvement in action. If a nursery attendant started a muscial toy in the corner of the room, all the little heads would turn in that direction and then the children would begin moving toward that toy. That would capture their interest for a short time. Then, if they heard a teacher reading a book in another part of the room, they would move in that direction to hear the story. A few would hold back, content to observe and not participate, but most of the children were eager to get involved. Little children love to be included in activities, to feel they are a part of the action. This desire for involvement can serve a parent well in daily biblical training.

And then little children learn by repetition. First they see, then they do, then they repeat what they have done. And through the repetition they imprint the learning in their minds.

Television commercials are frequently repeated because each time they are shown, they burrow a little deeper in the mind of the viewer. The same holds true for teaching spiritual truth. Repetition during the early years will imprint facts and truth on the mind of a child that will be impossible to erase.

Frances Xavier, a Jesuit missionary, said, "Give me the children until they are seven and anyone may have them afterwards."[1] The early teaching, consistent and repetitive, will last for a lifetime. Children may not understand all they are learning; in fact, it is certain they do not understand, but they accept and store away the teaching they receive.

Little children are vulnerable. They are unable to distinguish right from wrong. They only know they trust the teacher and they will accept everything that person says. Since children have no choice regarding their own parents, it becomes vital that the parents teach the right things in the right way.

Perhaps this is why Jesus spoke so forcefully to his disciples regarding the place of children in the kingdom of heaven. "And whoever welcomes a little child like this in my name welcomes me. But if anyone causes one of these little ones who believe in me to sin, it would be better for him to have a large millstone hung around his neck and to be drowned in the depths of the sea" (Matthew 18:5-6).

When the disciples became irritated with parents and children crowding around Jesus to seek his blessing, Jesus sharply rebuked his disciples and told them, "Let the little children come to me, and do not hinder them, for the kingdom of heaven belongs to such as these" (Matthew 19:14).

Because of the trusting, accepting response of children, Jesus used them as an example of the ideal member of the kingdom of God. Matthew 18:3-4: "I tell you the truth, unless you change and become like little children, you will never enter the kingdom of heaven. Therefore, whoever humbles himself like this child is the greatest in the kingdom of heaven."

Parents must decide the basic things they want to teach their children during the crucial preschool years. Because memories are short at this age and repetition is vital to effective learning, most of it will take place in the home. The Sunday school teachers can't do the job because they see the children only once a week for an hour. During the early years children miss Sunday school frequently because of colds and other childhood illnesses. If parents depended on the Sunday school for spiritual instruction, their children would receive only a few minutes per month. Sunday school is a fine supplement but cannot be the primary source of spiritual teaching.

Little children are capable of learning a number of basic lessons of the Christian life:

- A concept of God—who he is, his character, his attributes
- Love and respect for the Bible
- Prayer
- Kindness toward others
- Obedience to God and parents
- Common Bible characters

Several years ago one of our neighbors taught a class of preschoolers in the Sunday school at the church she attended. One day while talking with her, I asked her what she taught the children about God.

"Oh, I never talk about God," she answered. "We just talk about being kind, nice people. They are too young to grasp the concept of God."

How wrong she was. Children instinctively respond to the life of Jesus. They accept teaching about God without question. They pray willingly. They delight in hearing Bible stories and singing spiritual songs.

Preschool children respond more readily to biblical teaching if it comes in an attractive, enjoyable package. If parents are alert to and make use of the types of stimuli little children enjoy, they will notice a marked interest and anticipation when they announce that time has arrived for devotions.

Mark was one such little boy. When he was two years old, his parents felt the responsibility to regularly teach him biblical truth. Each day they read to him from a Bible storybook and prayed with him. But after a week or two he began to fidget and fuss when his father reached for the Bible storybook. His parents were dismayed when he pushed away the book and wiggled away to play with his toys.

Mark's mother checked with his Sunday school teacher and found that Mark was attentive and cooperative when he could see and participate in the learning process. Mark's mother made a few puppets from some small pieces of fabric. She invested in some pictures from the local Christian Bible bookstore. Mark's father drew some simple pictures with chalk and grease pencils to illustrate the stories he was reading.

They discussed the length of the devotional time and decided to cut it from fifteen minutes to three or four minutes. Each day they used a different visual aid to tell Mark a Bible story. On days when his interest was high, they continued for another minute or two, but always kept the time under five minutes. They prayed only briefly with him, or let him pray. When they sang a song, it was short and usually included actions. Soon Mark began to ask for "devos" at other times throughout the day.

Mark's parents found that with very little effort and time on their part, their son's interest in learning spiritual things was aroused, and they found the satisfaction of effectively communicating with him.

Try some of the following methods to keep the attention of your preschooler and to teach him the things of God.

Use lots of visual aids. Let your child touch, handle, investigate, and squeeze the aids you use to teach him. Use puppets, flannelgraph, blocks—anything that he can touch. Don't be afraid the child will ruin the equipment you use. You can always replace or mend the visual aids. Let the child learn by doing. If you can't find any aids, at least use your hands or your whole body to illustrate the story you are telling.

Use physical closeness during devotions. Hold your child on your lap or let him sit close to you. In a small way this will help your child associate the concept of God with love and care and closeness. Create an atmosphere of enjoyment and eagerness.

Avoid scolding and quarreling during devotions. If a child needs correction, remove him from the family circle and take care of it privately rather than having friction and fussing during the devotional time. If the presentations you make to the children are interesting and they are permitted to participate, you will find that your children will rarely need correction.

Keep it short. For children under two years old, two to three minutes should be enough. When they are three to five years old, five minutes will do. You can make your children sit through longer times, but you may lose the benefit. It is far better to include well-planned, quick presentations than to drag out a poorly planned devotional time. If your children are particularly tired, cut it even shorter. Pray briefly and sing a song. The content of your times may vary, but you will continue the consistency without overburdening the child when he isn't in condition to listen.

Continue supportive teaching throughout the day. Sing the songs you are emphasizing in devotions. Repeat the story. Mention the prayer requests again. Verbally reinforce what you have taught during the devotional time.

However, withhold the visual aids that you have used. Keep them particularly for the time when you are together as a family. Make them special. Allowing the child to play with them during the day will remove their intrigue as a teaching tool.

During the preschool years, much of your spiritual training will be done at times other than family devotions—as you take a walk together, ride in the car, and tuck the child into bed. But structured devotions will establish a pattern that will expand and develop as they grow older.

Your toddlers are ready to learn. They will respond to all you teach them about the Lord. A small investment of time and preparation on your part will reap dividends for years to come.

NOTES

1. Raymond S. Moore and Dorothy N. Moore, *Better Late than Early: A New Approach to Your Child's Education* (New York: E. T. Dutton and Company, Inc., 1975), page 77.

Suggested Resources

Bible Story Book

Egermeier, Elsie. *Egermeier's Favorite Bible Stories.* Anderson, Indiana: Warner Press, 1979.

Additional Reading

Arch Books Aloud, books and tapes. St. Louis, Missouri: Concordia Publishing House, 1979.

Beers, V. Gilbert. *Through Golden Windows.* Chicago: Moody Press, 1975.

Runyon, Leilah E. *I Learn to Read About Jesus.* Cincinnati, Ohio: The Standard Publishing Co., 1962.

8 Tweens

ELEMENTARY SCHOOL-AGE children are a delight for parents to work with spiritually. Tots charm us and teenagers challenge us, but tweens offer us the most gratifying opportunity to teach without resistance and to influence without rejection. They enjoy involvement, action, and learning.

They grasp much more than preschoolers but have not yet developed the indifference that some teenagers show. Family devotions with junior age children satisfy and delight parents as they see their children enjoying the things of God.

One Christmas Eve, Jerry and I washed the dinner dishes while the children made final preparations for their devotional presentation. They called us to the living room where they staged a pageant. Steve held center stage as Joseph, gowned in an old bathrobe and bath towel turban. One daughter played Mary. Our youngest child was squeezed into a doll cradle assuming the role of the baby Jesus. Various visiting cousins were pressed into service as shepherds and wise men. The tableau was complete. Steve read the nativity story from the book of Luke while the other members of the scene tried to look dignified. Another child prayed. Then the children led in singing a few Christmas carols. Some recited poems or pieces that they had learned about Christmas. The parents watching and the children participating enjoyed the devotional immensely.

For several years when our children were in elementary

school, they made elaborate preparations for similar Christmas devotions. We were sorry to see them lose interest in these performances when they reached the teen years and considered themselves too sophisticated to dress up in Dad's old bathrobes, wind towels around their heads, and put dish towels on the dog to simulate sheep.

Children from ages six to twelve are moving through a period of life when they experience varied and rapid changes. They enter school which is their first major exposure to life outside the home. Never again will the parents completely control the influences that shape their thoughts and actions. From then on, teachers and classmates will sway their thoughts and value judgments.

Relating

Tweens experience a gradually expanding range of relationships through school, church activities, clubs, recreation, and sports. Their world broadens explosively within a few years' time. Girls giggle, boys wrestle, girls like clothes and sports, boys like adventures and sports. By the end of the tween years they acquire a budding interest in one another.

From sheltered, pampered preschoolers who always have a sympathetic, listening ear, they are thrust into a new world of activity, timetables, requirements, relationships, and just plain work.

Jack had looked forward to starting school for a couple of years. His older brother attended school and he wanted to go too. But at the end of the first day he came home crying.

"We have to sit still, Mom. Teacher said we had to listen. I don't want to go back there. I'm going to stay home and play."

Of course, Jack returned to school and eventually realized the benefits of sitting still and listening to the teacher. But often the reality of the requirements of the real world shock younger tweens.

Maturing

During these years children emerge strongly into the personalities they will possess as adults. As preschoolers they could restrict their interrelationships, for the most part, to understanding and tolerant family members and neighbors. But once the child ventures into the extended world of teachers and classmates, his personality must blend with a much wider range of people.

The tween child must learn to adapt and cooperate if he is to get along with others. Tweens learn to effectively express themselves and their feelings as their vocabulary develops and their emotions mature. Where they were once obligated to scream and cry to express frustration and indignation, they must now learn to verbally express their feelings. Of course, that process doesn't end with the tween years. Personal maturity is a lifelong process, and some people never do achieve it—as evidenced by slamming doors, loud noises, and cars careening down the highway barely under the control of an angry person.

Tweens are thrust into an environment that demands compromise and tact. Granted, these qualities do not suddenly appear when children enter school, as anyone knows who has seen a school playground during the recess hour and heard the dozens of conflicts in progress. But the process begins and children learn and adapt.

Thinking

These are the years when children develop independent thinking processes. They no longer accept as complete truth everything they are told. When they hear conflicting information, as they are bound to do, they side with one point of view and then buttonhole parents, friends, and teachers to agree with their opinion.

One of our children arrived home from school one day in a state of indignation.

"You seem upset," I told her.

"I am," she answered. "My friend said a bad word today and when I told her she shouldn't say that, she said bad words don't count unless you are mad and she wasn't mad. They do too count, don't they, Mom? Don't they?"

She felt strongly that her set of values had been attacked and she wanted reinforcement from me that she was right and her friend was wrong.

While children of this age are pliable and teachable, they are structuring their own set of guidelines and values, so it is a crucial time for parents to be alert to every possible chance to influence and guide their thinking and understanding of biblical principles.

They are developing the ability to think conceptually and will be making decisions regarding a number of crucial issues in their lives:

- Salvation
- Identifying publicly with Christ
- Honesty versus cheating and lying
- Industriousness versus laziness
- Obedience
- Loyalty
- Friendship

If parents are aware that the thinking processes are developing, then they can guide the decisions of their children and use the Scriptures to help them develop the right attitudes.

Learning

Children in the elementary school years are eager learners. They have a huge capacity for learning, and when properly motivated they can grasp a large amount of material.

Children will absorb far more information than their parents did simply because of the speed with which new frontiers of knowledge are opening. Space, science, biology, engineering, and nutrition are some of the fields of study that have developed rapidly in recent years.

Some school teachers have an instinctive ability to motivate children to learn, but others do not. Parents are the same, but Christian parents have the advantage of the indwelling Holy Spirit to give guidance and ingenuity to the spiritual teaching process.

Identifying

Tween children love to run in groups—they form clubs and secret organizations. They have "best friends" and "best, best friends." Although they may change "best friends" frequently, they are devotedly loyal while a pact lasts.

This group urge can be used to advantage during the devotional time with the entire family gathered around the Scriptures. Togetherness gives children a sense of completeness and security, and sets the right atmosphere for learning.

They appreciate regimentation and structure, so it seems natural to them that family devotions should be conducted on a regular basis. The key to keeping their interest is to vary the format of the devotions but not the regularity.

Children of this age enjoy telling stories. They repeat the details of events and happenings and stories. Encourage your children to retell the stories you have been reading in devotions. Have one child tell the story while another acts it out. Or tell the story together as a group—each family member adding one sentence at a time.

These children love to be physically active. They cannot sit still for extended periods of time. They run when they could walk, they hop and skip when a sedate pace would do, they jiggle and twist and squirm. And because they do, parents who keep devotions brisk and full of things for the children to do will find a happier response and far more effective learning.

When I asked my ten-year-old daughter what she liked best about family devotions she answered, "I like it when we have flannelgraph and I can help. No, no wait. I know. I like it best when we have sword drills and I try to find the verse first."

Notice that she selected activities in which she could participate and be active.

Spiritual Value in Tween Devotions

Many children in the middle years reach a point of decision concerning Christ. In strong Christian homes where biblical teaching has been consistent, a child may indicate a desire to receive Christ when he is still of preschool age. If your child does make an early decision, help him to the best of his comprehension. A child's response to God is a simple thing and God will meet your child at the point of his understanding.

When children reach school age and acquire a deeper understanding of spiritual things, parents should present the gospel clearly and then offer the child the opportunity to respond. To insure that the child does not misunderstand, use a week of devotional times to lay the groundwork for specific questions.

The first day read John 3:1-21 in *The Living Bible.*

The next day present the Four Spiritual Laws or a similar explanation of the gospel. Together read through the presentation, asking the child to read portions consistent with his ability.

Read Isaiah 53 another day, perhaps with a cross of sticks and a roughly shaped crown of thorns for emphasis (if you have the proper bushes and trees nearby).

Then at a private time, perhaps his bedtime, or anytime you are with the child alone, ask him if he has received Christ and if he would like to do it now. Resist any urge to pressure the child. The decision must be his.

If your child tells you he has received Christ, this is an ideal time to give him scriptural proof that what he has done assures his eternity with God. Thank God with the child that together you are a part of the kingdom of God, and ask God to help your child grow into a mature Christian.

Through these years you will find many chances to show your children the relevance of the Bible to their daily lives.

If you get a call from your child's teacher saying your child has lied or cheated in school, help him by showing him a Scripture passage that details the seriousness of his actions.

If your child seems fearful, emphasize passages or characters in the Bible who faced fear and conquered it with God's help. Use the story of Shadrack, Meshack and Abednego, or Daniel, or the disciples on the lake during the storm (see Daniel 3, Daniel 6, Mark 6:45-52). Include short verses like Psalm 4:8 or 56:3, or Isaiah 41:10. Help the child to memorize these verses and encourage him to repeat them when he feels a wave of fear coming over him.

Many other situations allow parents to gear the family devotions to the needs of their children:

- Family conflicts
- Broken friendships
- Doubting God's love
- Questioning the truth of Scripture

During the middle years parents can whet the spiritual appetites of their children for God's word and a relationship with him. This will influence their responses to God during their teen years. If a positive, appreciative attitude to the Bible is established during the elementary school years, a child will enter his teen years ready to develop a continuing relationship with God.

Children of this age can begin to comprehend and appreciate deep spiritual truth. They can understand basic Bible doctrines such as salvation, spiritual maturity, grace, God, and Satan.

They can learn more about prayer and find real joy when God answers. But they can also accept answers that they did not ask for or expect, understanding that Romans 8:28 is true: "And we know that in all things God works for the good of those who love him, who have been called according to his purpose."

Children in the middle years still remain fairly available to parents' schedules. Although their activities and involvements outside of the home are increasing, they are dependent on parents to make most decisions regarding their schedules. Therefore, parents can control family members' use of time and the frequency of devotions.

Scriptural teaching at any age is important, but crucially so during the middle years. Parents would do well to cancel activities that conflict with family devotions. Children can enter sports, take music lessons, and attend special events throughout life, but if parents allow other activities to crowd aside spiritual training, they cancel the most important part of a child's life. The opportunity to teach children spiritually at this tender age comes only once and then is gone forever. Make every effort during these years to draw the family together regularly for devotions.

Use teaching methods that interest children of this age.

They love competition. Use contests for Scripture memory or memorizing the books of the Bible in order. Award small, appropriate prizes of your choice. See that every child in the family is a winner. If the major winner gets a large reward, give the losers something smaller.

Vary your approach. Read, use visual aids, pictures, flannelgraph, and art work. Ask the children to plan and lead your devotions. Use a recorded Bible story. Ask them to role play. Use charades to quiz one another on Bible events and characters. Write and give simple tests on passages of Scripture you have been covering. Use Bible games, but select them carefully. Some are rather boring. Ask them to design plays or skits depicting Bible stories. Read a story and ask them to draw a picture of their interpretation of the story or a Bible truth. Use their Sunday school material to reinforce the teaching during a devotional time on Monday.

Emphasize prayer. Ask one of your older middle children to keep a prayer record book. Record requests in one column and answers in another. Record items for thanks.

Tweens love to participate. They enjoy helping and being in the center of activities. But they quickly forget unless teaching is reinforced, so plan to repeat frequently what you teach and share with them. You will have the satisfaction of seeing them develop a relationship with God that can carry through their teen years and on into adulthood.

Suggested Devotions for Tweens

Ten-day period

Emphasis: Importance of obedience to God

Day 1 Read Joshua 1:1-9 in *The Living Bible.* One parent read while the other shows a map of the described territory (many Bibles have maps).

Questions to ask:

What did the Lord mean when he told Joshua to be strong and courageous?

In what ways do we need to be strong or courageous?

Why is it so important to obey all of God's laws?
Note: If your children are unaccustomed to answering questions during devotions, you may have to supply correct answers for a few days. Always accept their answers without criticism, but be sure the correct answer is given either by them or you.
Prayer: Conversational prayer centered around obeying God's word and asking God for courage in everyday situations
Extra activity: Play an active outdoors game for ten minutes (frisbee, kickball, dodgeball).

Day 2 Read Egermeier's *Bible Story Book,* "Rahab Helps the Spies" (Joshua 1-2).
Role playing: As you read, let these characters pantomine the story: Joshua, two spies, and Rahab.
Prayer emphasis: personal needs (one child writing requests); missionaries (use pictures); conversational prayer.
Sing: "Trust and Obey."

Day 3 Read Egermeier's *Bible Story Book,* "Crossing the Jordan" (Joshua 3:1-5).
Prayer: father or mother only
Memory: Start Matthew 4:4.
Extra activity: Begin reading a "Danny Orlis" book or a short missionary biography.

Day 4 Read Egermeier's *Bible Story Book,* "Walls of Jericho" (Joshua 5:13-6:27). Use flannelgraph or standing figures.
Have children act out the march around Jericho as you read and show pictures.
Prayer: your church, pastors, Sunday school teachers, personal needs
Memory: Continue working on Matthew 4:4.
Extra activity: Continue reading in "Danny Orlis" or a short missionary biography.

Day 5 Read Hebrews 11:30 *(The Living Bible).*
Questions:

Why did God tell about Jericho in the New Testament?
Whose faith brought the walls down?
What is faith?
In what ways can we show our faith?
Prayer: Open in conversational prayer.
Sing: Teach "Faith of our Fathers."
Extra activity: Continue reading.

Day 6 Read Joshua 7:1-8, 8:18-26. Achan's sin. During the reading, have a child place flannelgraph figures on the background.
Questions:
Why was Achan's sin so bad?
How can the sin of one person affect many other Christians today?
What can we do to avoid sin that will hurt us and other people?
Prayer: Father leads the family in corporate confession and prayer for holiness of life.
Extra activity: Continue reading.

Day 7 Read Joshua 8:30-35, "Joshua Builds God's Altar." Use flannelgraph or pictures.
Prayer: time of thanksgiving for Scripture, God's goodness
Memory: Review Matthew 4:4.
Extra activities: Continue reading; tell riddles.

Day 8 Read Joshua 9:3-27, "Joshua Tricked by Strangers." Father—read part of Joshua, plus narration. Mother—read part of strangers.
Prayer: conversational prayer for family or missionaries (Use pictures if possible.)
Memory: Review Matthew 4:4.

Day 9 Spend entire time singing. Be prepared with suggestions. Ask your children what they want to sing. Include some songs with motions.

Day 10 Use Egermeier's *Bible Story Book,* "Sun and Moon Stood Still"—Joshua 10-12. Show encyclopedia pictures of sun's orbit. Discuss the miracle involved in changing

the pattern of the natural order of the universe.
Question:
How does God answer our prayers?
Prayer: Pray for some of the big things you have on your prayer list, or think of some big requests to ask God for.
Memory: Offer a reward to all who can correctly quote Matthew 4:4.
Extra activity: Continue story reading.

Suggested Resources

Bible Story Book

Egermeier, Elsie. *Egermeier's Bible Story Book*. New ed. Anderson, Indiana: Warner Press, 1969.

Additional Reading

Arch Books Aloud, books and tapes. St. Louis, Missouri: Concordia Publishing House, 1979.

Barrett, Ethel. *Gregory the Grub, Buzzy Bee, Blister Lamb,* books and tapes. Glendale, California: Regal Books, A Division of Gospel Light Publications, 1978.

Bible Games

Who Am I?, Vols. 1 and 2. *What Am I?,* Vol. 1. Grand Rapids, Michigan: Zondervan Publishing House, 1965.

Visual Aids

Pict-O-Graph, flannelgraph series. Cincinnati, Ohio: The Standard Publishing Co..

9 Teens

IF TODDLERS ARE charming and tween children are spirited learners, then teenagers are challenging—in a positive way. Spiritual training for teenagers requires creativity and ingenuity. Gone are the days of picture books and puppets. Instead, parents have a thinking, responding, independent fellow Christian to train and help.

Joyce returned from school one afternoon and told her mother, "I think I'll study psychology and anthropology in college. My teacher tells me that way I'll be able to figure out people."

Wisely, Joyce's mother didn't tell her she could find out from the Bible. She listened to Joyce and let her talk through her new interest. Then she planned devotional times that stressed the way Jesus interacted with people. Eventually Joyce began to see the effective ways Jesus related to various people. Her mother suggested additional reading by a prominent Christian psychologist. Today Joyce is in college studying Christian education and psychology. She feels God is leading her into counseling.

The exciting part of having teenagers in your home is watching their spiritual development, seeing them mature to the point where they rely on their parents, not for teaching, but for fellowship. As every parent with teens knows, we also struggle, pray, and cry for them as they go through this process. Every Christian parent longs to see a child who can sustain himself spiritually, who values Christian principles and cherishes his walk with God. But we find a significant gap between the early years of adolescence and the time when the teenager leaves home with both parent and child confident of the child's spiritual strength.

The adolescent enters the years before his independence with hopes and fears. With varying degrees of struggle he reaches for independence and self-sufficiency. Some teens ease into adulthood with few emotional ripples, while others barge into independence, scattering emotionally wrecked people (usually their parents) in their wake. Still others make the transition painfully, slowly, and awkwardly, suffering endless hours of introspection, self-analysis, and self-criticism.

Christian teens follow this process, too. The Holy Spirit in their lives prevents some of the trauma, but they are, after all, human beings and develop in much the same way as other teenagers. Parents need to be prepared spiritually and mentally for the impact that teenagers will have on their lives.

One of the major tasks an adolescent faces is developing his self-concept. "The central theme of adolescence is that of *identity*, coming to know who one is, what one believes in and values, what one wants to accomplish and get out of life."[1]

Every adult has passed through these years and knows the inner feelings of change, seeking, longing, and the deep need for a sense of belonging, acceptance, approval, and affection.

> Writers on the subject of adolescence . . . have been struck by the adolescent's agonies of self-consciousness, his preoccupation with who he is and where he belongs. They have noted his proneness to idealism, religious conversion, moodiness and changes of mood, to feelings that life is futile, and to rebellion and iconoclasm. Adolescence has come to be known as a period of . . . "storm and stress." Needless to say, this inner turmoil finds external expression, and the adults who have to deal with adolescents come in for their share of turmoil too.[2]

Our culture gives teenagers no basic pattern for identity. Increasingly, we find that the American ideals and traditions have broken down and social restraint and moral values have been removed or ignored. Apart from a stable family and a strong church, there are few available structures in society with which a teenager can identify.

Of course, this is not a new phenomenon. It has happened many times before in many cultures, but Christian parents do possess the answer to their teenager's quest for identity. The dilemma is how to communicate that answer.

As our children pass through these years, we have the fine opportunity to build on the teaching that we have done through the toddler and middle years. The training and teaching we instilled in our children should mature into their own convictions. With some help from us, our teenagers will find self-worth, identity, and fulfillment in their relationship with God.

However, even if you haven't built spiritually through their earlier years, opportunities abound for you to help your teenager's transition to a spiritually satisfying adulthood. Never hesitate to begin training at any age. You cannot retrace your steps, but you can begin where you are to start guiding your teenager's thoughts and habits.

An acquaintance of Jerry's recently became a Christian in his late thirties. As he began to grow, he wanted to teach and lead his teenage children. He finally asked them if he could read the Bible to them regularly. They nonchalantly answered, "I guess so." Then he asked, "Do you know anything about the Bible?" "No," they replied. So he began to explain that the Bible had two major sections, the Old and New Testaments, and there were sixty-six books or letters. He began where *he* was and started where *they* were. It's never too late.

Teenagers are developing a finely tuned ability to think conceptually, and this increases with their age. They do not have full emotional maturity, but parents can appeal to them on the basis of their ability to reason. However, always remember as you present matters of spiritual importance to your teenager, that faith and belief play a strong part in their lives. We cannot explain everything. Some spiritual truths we accept by faith, such as:

- The existence of God
- The certainty of heaven
- The miraculous creation of the world
- The resurrection of Jesus Christ
- The assurance of life after death

These beliefs are based on the word, not just blind faith, but faith nevertheless. Parents can allow the Holy Spirit to do a work of confirming, through faith, the reality of the things which are unseen. "Now faith is being sure of what we hope for and certain of what we do not see" (Hebrews 11:1).

The Christian walk becomes a combination of faith and intelligent reasoning for teenagers. Parents can guide that development and try to help their teenagers balance faith and reason.

The most important factor in dealing with teenagers is to cultivate an awareness of their thinking and their needs. Then we must help them apply Scripture to meet those needs.

Teenagers need the biblical basis for dealing with the pressures and everyday occurrences in their lives. Parents should consider emphasizing some of the following topics in the devotional times with their adolescent children.

Doctrine. Do your teens know major Bible doctrines such as salvation, the deity of Jesus Christ, the fellowship of believers, and the second coming of Christ?

Resisting temptation. Teens experience a great deal of peer pressure. Rather than speaking negatively regarding the pressures to sin, parents can stress the strength we have from God in resisting temptation.

Developing their own convictions. If based on Bible principles and knowledge, teenagers can develop their own convictions regarding a great many issues of life:

- Personal responsibility
- Work
- Relationships
- Friendship
- Church

- Sex
- Marriage
- Honesty
- Finances
- Giving
- Personal holiness

Parents need to recognize some of the changes that will happen in the family devotional patterns when their children reach the teen years.

Devotions may be less frequent. Most families' varying and hectic schedules simply do not permit the entire family to gather every day. School schedules, sports, lessons, and social activities combine to split the family. Some families can get together only a few times each week, or even once each week.

Teenagers don't appreciate being told anything. They want to discover for themselves. Parents can aid this discovery process by involving teenagers as much as possible in the devotional times. The use of Bible studies, Scripture memory programs, quizzes, and discussions promote personal involvement.

It's important at this age to keep the time brisk, although occasionally a devotional time will assume a mellow, meditative, reflective quality when everyone in the family contributes in a quiet way. More than at any other time of conducting family devotions, parents need sensitivity to the moods of their children and should then flow with that mood. If the teenagers are in a hurry to go somewhere, let them know they won't be detained by the devotions. If they have no pressing commitments, make them aware that they can participate for longer periods.

Since devotions probably won't be daily, it is imperative to plan well for each time. Don't force participation by your teenagers. If they don't enter a discussion, allow them that privilege, but do insist on their physical presence. Review the type of devotions you are having and try to make them as appealing as possible. As parents, we are competing with television and other exciting diversions for our teens' attention.

Lay aside family frictions during devotions. Biblical fellowship and teaching can't take place in an atmosphere of hostility and tension. Resolve to avoid quarreling and controversy. If dissension crops up, stop the devotions and try again another time.

Avoid ridicule or criticism of your teenagers' ideas or prayers. Parents are often amazed at the amount they can learn from their children if they will listen to what they share. Set a positive tone. Help your teenagers feel good about themselves.

If you are having a Bible study discussion and they offer a completely wrong answer, tell them you appreciate the answer and ask for any further thoughts. If need be, gently bring the right answer into focus. If your children feel threatened or ridiculed when they participate, they will stop saying anything.

What if you have already made some of these mistakes and your children resist a devotional time? Explain to them the wrong approach you have used and tell them you intend to conduct family devotions differently. Then ask them for their participation, help, and suggestions.

This is a wonderful age to emphasize Scripture as it relates to everyday living. Try to focus biblical application on specific issues your children are facing. They might include:

- Ethics
- Sexual morality
- Dating procedures
- Entertainments
- Will of God
- Death
- Suicide
- Worth of the individual
- Attitude toward education
- Cheating

Learn to read the signals that your teenagers give. Are they always friendly and cooperative? Deep within, they doubtless have questions and concerns that may not manifest themselves in open rebellion.

Are they hostile and discourteous at home? Try to determine why. What underlying reasons can you find for such behavior? It may be, of course, just plain sin. A teenager may react negatively if he is under pressure from studies, if he has quarreled with his best friend, if he feels disliked by a teacher, or if he feels guilty about some act.

Keep communications low-key but open. That will help foster the trust a teenager needs in order to share difficult situations with parents. Then parents can meet these difficulties in a spiritual way with spiritual answers.

On Their Own

By the time teenagers leave home, they should be established in a pattern of personal devotions. Or perhaps we should say, they should have been introduced to a pattern of personal devotions. Whether they follow such a pattern is their decision.

Many children begin reading the Bible on their own before they reach their teen years. If they have not, however, they should be starting some program of their own, however irregular it might be in the beginning.

Suggest a simple plan. Most Bibles have divisions within the chapters. Suggest that your teenager begin in the Gospel of Mark and read the first portion of the first chapter. Give him a small notebook divided into two parts. In the front he can jot down any thoughts that occur to him while he is reading. In the second section he can keep a record of prayer requests and answers. If he has observed this procedure in devotions, or has seen his parents using such a plan, it will come more naturally to him.

Encourage him to look for a few things as he is reading. Are there any promises in the passage to claim? Are there any sins to avoid? Is there a command to obey?

Reinforce personal devotions by asking your teenager to share occasionally during family devotions what he is learning or praying for in his personal devotions. Some teenagers may be reluctant to do this, and if so, don't force the issue. But in a tactful way, let your teenager know that while devotions promote personal growth and a living relationship with God, that relationship should naturally and freely affect those around him.

Set a tone in your home which encourages the natural and regular sharing of spiritual matters. Speak freely of your own prayer concerns and praises, or of the reading you have recently done and how it affected you. That will establish a direction for your children to follow. Occasionally ask what they are learning in their devotions.

Then pray, pray, pray for your teenagers that they will maintain a close, sweet fellowship with the Lord. You may be the only person in the world praying for your child. Ask God to do whatever is necessary in his life to give him a deep hunger for a relationship with God. Sometimes it may be well to pray through the prayer that Solomon prayed for his son in Proverbs 2:1-8:

> My son, if you accept my words and store up my commands within you, turning your ear to wisdom and applying your heart to understanding, and if you call out for insight and cry aloud for understanding, and if you look for it as for silver and search for it as for hidden treasure, then you will understand the fear of the Lord and find the knowledge of God. For the Lord gives wisdom, and from his mouth come knowledge and understanding. He holds victory in store for the upright, he is a shield to those whose walk is blameless, for he guards the course of the just and protects the way of his faithful ones.

One of the greatest frustrations concerned parents encounter with a teenager is to know what they are *really* thinking. They bottle things up in their minds. They fear sharing what they really think. Here much of our impact and encouragement requires a step of faith, often without receiving much feedback. But it will bear fruit.

> But as for you, continue in what you have learned and have become convinced of, because you know those from whom you learned it, and how from infancy you have known the holy Scriptures, which are able to make you wise for salvation through faith in Christ Jesus (2 Timothy 3:14-15).

Teens undergo the most significant physical and emotional changes they will ever encounter as they enter puberty and become adults. Use your family devotions to meet them at their point of need. For instance, common teen experiences can be used as follows:

- *Peer pressure*—Discuss peer pressure on the basis of Joseph's brothers, the crowd calling for Jesus' crucifixion, Paul's companions, Daniel and his friends, and specific verses on developing one's own convictions.
- *Fear*—Use examples of the disciples in the storm, Moses before Pharaoh, and Paul in prison.
- *Puberty*—Use this as a reason to teach on sex, marriage, and morality.
- *Dating*—Again discuss God's standards for relationships with the opposite sex.

It is much easier to approach these issues when they come in the normal *planned* course of devotions than to speak of them only in a crisis situation.

We have found the teen years to be the most fun and fulfilling of any age of our children. They are adults and can communicate as adults. They begin to relate as peers and to think for themselves. They begin to evaluate the consistency of their parents and the reality of their own commitment. What a great time for sharing in their growth through family devotions. You will be surprised at the discussions that develop from your family time together.

NOTES

1. L. Joseph Stone and Joseph Church, *Childhood and Adolescence: A Psychology of the Growing Person* (New York: Random House, 1968), page 437.
2. Ibid., page 435.

Suggested Resources

Additional Reading

Canfield, Carolyn L. *One Vision Only*. Chicago: Moody Press, 1959.

Colson, Charles W. *Born Again*. Old Tappan, New Jersey: Chosen Books, Fleming H. Revell Company, 1976.

Elliott, Elisabeth. *Through Gates of Splendor*. New York: Harper and Brothers, Publishers, 1957.

Taylor, Mrs. Howard. *Behind the Ranges*. Chicago: Moody Press, 1964.

General Reading

Butler, John. *Christian Ways to Date, Go Steady and Break Up*. Cincinnati, Ohio: The Standard Publishing Co., 1978.

Schaeffer, Francis A. *How Should We Then Live?* Old Tappan, New Jersey: Fleming H. Revell Company, 1976.

Trobisch, Walter. *I Loved a Girl*. New York: Harper and Row, 1965.

10 Special Occasions

EVERY FAMILY EXPERIENCES occasions and events which give natural opportunities for teaching biblical principles and truths. With a little preparation, parents can take advantage of these times to turn the children's attention toward particular truths and ideas. Many of these events occur on an annual basis, and the same teaching can be repeated year after year without becoming tedious.

Usually we are aware of these events and occasions for some time before they occur. That gives us ample time to think about the teaching we want to present to our children. Only a few minutes of preparation will be needed to give children a lasting impression of the importance of an occasion.

Consider the following events that allow specific, concentrated teaching.

Weddings

Last summer friends of ours were married in a nearby town. Our family dressed up for the occasion and drove the short distance to the wedding. As we returned that evening, we talked about God's plan for marriage in Ephesians 5 and prayed for our newly-married friends. That was our devotional time.

Use weddings and anniversaries to explain God's perspective on marriage, his purpose, and his plan for families. These occasions may also be used as a springboard to discuss dating, sex, and the complimentary roles of male and female in life.

Use passages such as:

- Genesis 2:18-25; the first wedding
- John 2:1-11; Jesus' attendance at a wedding
- Ephesians 5:22-33; God's plan for marriage

On your anniversary dig out your wedding pictures. Prepare to hear your children explode with laughter over the clothing and hairstyles. Tell your children about your wedding. Increase their security by reassuring them of your continuing love for each other and for them. Thank God together for forming your family in the special way that he has done.

Thanksgiving

Each year at Thanksgiving our family gathers for a time of praise and appreciation to the Lord. Sometimes our sessions are general, but often we concentrate on specifics.

- What we appreciate about other family members
- Spiritual blessings of the past year
- Friends we are thankful for
- Material comforts and enjoyments
- Extended family and their meaning to us
- Difficulties in which God helped us

If we have guests, and we usually do, we include them in our time of praise and thanks. Often we sing, perhaps ending our meal by singing the Doxology and then having a conversational time of thanksgiving in prayer.

Check your encyclopedia for the origins of the Thanksgiving holiday and read, or explain, the details to your family. Use any available pictures. Tell them of the gratitude of the early settlers at Plymouth, Massachusetts. During their first dreadful winter there, nearly half of their number died. Yet they organized a day of thanksgiving.

Tell your children that President Lincoln, in 1863, formally declared that on the last Thursday of November the nation should annually pause to give thanks to God for his bounty and goodness to us.

Christmas

The advent of Christ presents probably the most varied and extended opportunity of any special occasion that occurs during the year.

Children love the Christmas season. Our children often begin playing Christmas records long before Thanksgiving. The anticipation and enjoyment children experience during Christmas can be used to draw their attention to the true importance of the season.

Use the traditional advent wreath or log for an extended weekly time of discussion and meditation covering the Old Testament predictions concerning the Messiah, through his birth recorded in the New Testament.

Our church bulletin includes a weekly insert during advent that gives suggestions for family activities. You could check your church library for ideas, or your Christian bookstore would have books supplying similar information.

Jerry and the children quite often make our advent logs. Simply split a log and drill holes into it to hold five candles. The children gather greens and berries to decorate the log. Light one candle each of the four Sundays preceding Christmas. The last candle is lit on Christmas Day.

Use music lavishly during your Christmas devotions. As your children grow, insure their knowledge of familiar Christmas carols and songs. Learn new ones together. Include some contemporary Christmas music in your singing and listening.

During one of your devotions talk about gift giving. Tell your children that you enjoy giving and receiving gifts, but emphasize that Jesus Christ, the greatest gift of all, is the center of Christmas. It may take years before children see the receiving of gifts in its true perspective, but continue to emphasize the preeminence of Christ in your family's celebrations.

Encourage your children to memorize verses or passages

that relate directly to the coming of Christ, such as Isaiah 9:6 and Luke 2:4-7. Or be ambitious and memorize Matthew 1:18 through Matthew 2:12. You might make a family project of memorizing all of the passages together.

Use some of your devotional time to prepare small gifts for neighbors and friends.

Fourth of July

On a recent Fourth of July, only two of our children were at home. Each had invited a guest to spend the holiday with us. After a leisurely dinner, punctuated by pops and cracks as the neighborhood children exploded firecrackers, we read a Scripture portion together, Jerry prayed, then I opened the encyclopedia and showed the children a replica of the Declaration of Independence.

We read excerpts from the accompanying article, took special note of John Hancock's overly large signature, and spent some time talking about the men who courageously struggled to gain independence for the colonies.

We speculated on what our life would be like if we were still a part of the British Empire. We discussed, too, some of the benefits and privileges of being a part of this country, at this point in history. Our guests entered enthusiastically into the discussion.

Interest remained keen throughout the conversation which lasted about ten minutes. We then went outdoors to celebrate by adding a few fireworks and sparklers to the miniature explosions already in progress around us.

Birth

Are you expecting a baby? Have some friends just had a baby? Use the opportunity to teach your children about God's view of each human life. You can also include some facts regarding sex which are consistent with the ages and understanding of your children.

When baby announcements arrive in the mail, bring them to your devotional time and let your children know of the birth. Use part of the devotional time to read Psalm 127:3-5 to show your children the blessing God intends each new child to be. Ask one of the children to pray for the parents and the new baby. Prepare and wrap a gift for the baby and the mother.

Job Changes or Moves

Changes unsettle and disturb children, especially during their pre-adolescent and teen years. They feel threatened and insecure because of the disruption in their lives.

When our second child left for college, our youngest child felt bereft and alone. They had been very close friends. We spent several weeks of special concentration on her needs until she once again felt personally secure and convinced of God's goodness in allowing her sister to go to college.

In our mobile society, families must often move and make adjustments when the father or mother accepts a new job. Such an event gives parents an opportunity to share with their children how God has given direction, to pray together regarding the move, and to share fears, aspirations, and hopes about the new situation.

Use part of your devotional time to bring to the surface problems relating to the changes. Ask your children what they fear about the change. Explain what the new job will mean and what will happen step by step in their new situation.

Pray with them about everything, including matters that may seem trivial to you, but which loom large in their thinking.

- Where will the dog sleep?
- Will I have a room of my own?
- What will my school be like?
- Will I have new friends?
- Will I ever see my old friends again?
- How long will it take to get to the new house?
- Why does Dad have to take the new job?
- Where will we go to church?
- Do they have McDonald's hamburgers there?
- Does it snow there?

Of course, you will be discussing these questions often with your children throughout the days and weeks before your move, but use your devotional time for specific prayer and detailed explanations. Emphasize positive benefits in the change.

- God has given Dad a better job.
- God has provided indications of why we should move (name them).
- God can do even more for our family in the new location. (There's an exciting church to join, and lots of friendly neighbors. We can ski. We will have a bigger house. The school has a soccer team.)

Leaving is hard but sometimes the hard times are the best times. God is sovereign over all of life and can turn any difficult situation into something good.

Our last move took place as a result of a job change for Jerry. Since it was our only major move in several years, our children were understandably apprehensive. Kristin expressed repeated fears that she would never find friends in Seattle. Knowing her open, friendly personality, we were convinced she would quickly make friends, but we put "new friends for Kris" as a top priority item on the family's prayer list.

The day we moved into our house, she roamed around the neighborhood and met *eleven* children. Now, when her faith seems shaky, or she voices fears, we remind her of that answer to prayer a few years ago.

Use Scripture readings that tell of people who made drastic changes in location and jobs and enjoyed the blessing of God.

- Noah—farmer to shipbuilder
- Abraham—city dweller to nomad
- Jacob—mother's pet to farm manager
- Joseph—privileged son to slave to national ruler
- Moses—royal son to shepherd to national leader
- Ruth—interracial wife to widow to ancestor of Christ
- Deborah—housewife to national leader

Birthdays

Most families prepare some recognition and celebration for family members when a birthday rolls around. Birthdays give an opportunity to recognize a family member as someone special and loved.

Plan a time of remembrance and review for each child on his birthday—a celebration that allows more than a flurry of cake, ice cream, and gaily wrapped gifts.

Assemble a picture review of the life of your child. It need not be extensive. Five or ten photographs would give a fine view of the child's growth, development, and special activities.

Review for the child your delight and pleasure on the day he was born. Tell him of his grandparents' pleased reactions to his arrival. If you thanked God for him and prayed for him, tell him so. Children long remember the affirmation and affection expressed by their parents in just such a birthday celebration.

Always pray aloud for the child, thanking God for his life and asking for God's direction and blessing in the coming year.

Easter

Use this joyous, triumphant celebration to strengthen your children's understanding and belief in the redeeming death and resurrection of Jesus Christ.

Begin a few weeks before Easter to read Scripture passages that detail the final week of Jesus' life, such as John 18-20, Luke 22-24, and Mark 14-16. On Easter Sunday read the stirring account of the resurrection from John 20.

Help your children form a cross of sticks tied together with string and a crown of twigs woven together to serve as a centerpiece for your Easter table.

Initiate a discussion concerning what our lives would be like if Jesus had *not* lived and died and risen again for our redemption. Then thank God together for the work of Jesus Christ for us.

If you are not certain that your children have made a personal commitment to Jesus Christ, this would be an ideal time to stress the reason for Christ's death and resurrection, and then to ask your children if they want to receive him as their personal Savior.

With these suggestions in mind, develop and use specific teaching on other occasions that are special for your family.

- Family reunions
- Memorial Day
- Baptism
- Death of a friend or family member
- Starting school
- Missionary visitors
- Spiritual birthdays
- Vacations
- Illness of friends or relatives
- Graduation

Children love special occasions and respond positively when they realize devotions contain something unusual in the way of emphasis. Sometimes you will find special occasions occurring every few weeks. That may seem often to you, but your children will be delighted with the variation, and you will discover a renewed interest and zest in your devotional times.

11 Special Problems

EVEN WHEN PARENTS make sincere attempts at enlivening and sustaining family devotions, problems will develop. Expect problems and don't be intimidated by them. Try various solutions, fresh ideas, and compromises. Eventually you will discover something that will work for your family.

Discuss devotions with your children. Seek their evaluations and their suggestions. Any child over five or six years of age will be able to tell you clearly what he likes and doesn't like about your family devotions.

Here are some typical questions that seem to come up most often.

My husband wants me to do all the planning and sharing during devotions. I thought the husband was to be the spiritual leader. How do we handle that?

Both parents should support the family devotions one hundred percent, but usually one will have the interest, the creativity, and the *time* to plan and prepare. Usually the mother will be the one to do the preparation. Some men will have fresh, stimulating ideas and will make excellent plans, but we have found that most often the mothers do the groundwork.

Because of my interest in this area of our children's development, I have done most of the thinking and preparation and then discussed the materials and plans with my husband. He has readily accepted my suggestions and relied on my ideas. Sometimes he leads and sometimes I do, but the important thing is that our children understand we are totally in agreement on the devotional time.

Help your husband by making some plans and gathering the materials you will use and then talk them over with him. Together you can decide who is going to lead and make the presentation.

We always have Bible reading and prayer around the table after dinner. Our children are restless and often quarrelsome during this time. What could we do?

Surprise them! Take their minds off each other and focus their attention on what you are trying to teach. After your next dinner together, announce to your children that you are going outdoors. Take them to the backyard or a nearby park. Have them lie down on the grass. Read part of the creation account in Genesis 1 and then ask them to name everything they can see that God created. Then pray briefly, thanking God for his creative power, the beauty that surrounds us, and his amazing diversity (in simple terms, of course).

Children love changes and surprises. You don't have to be original every day, but an occasional change will help you keep your children's interest and attention.

It seems to me that our family devotions are negative times of family interaction instead of positive communication. Our children criticize each other during discussions and then I scold them. What could I do to change that?

Ask yourself, Am I legalistic, preachy, scolding, stuffy, or critical during devotions? Or do my children see that I do love God's word and want to learn together with them?

For a time, you do all the talking during the devotional time. Don't invite your children to participate. Use visual aids to keep their interest. After you sense that the atmosphere has changed, include your children once again in the discussions.

When you are the only one speaking during devotions, keep

the time brief so you don't lose your children's attention. By any possible means keep the devotional time a positive, happy time of learning and interaction.

Our family devotions seem isolated from real life. We never talk about God except when we read the Bible together and pray. What could be wrong?

Children must learn that spiritual values permeate every area of life and that as parents we are aware of God's presence and work in our daily lives. It helps if you remember throughout the day what you have read and prayed about with your children the last time you had devotions together. Bring it up again at an appropriate time. It will take a little practice to make it sound genuine, but keep at it until it becomes a natural and frequent part of daily conversation.

You might say things like, "Do you remember praying this morning that Grandma would get well? She called today and she is feeling much better."

"I've been thinking about that verse we read today in Ephesians where it says we should be kind to one another. I'm afraid I wasn't kind to you today when I told you to hurry up and get in the car when we were going to your piano lessons and I called you a slowpoke. I am sorry about that. Will you forgive me?"

"I was looking in the Bible encyclopedia today and found a picture of the place where Jesus fed the five thousand people. Do you remember reading that story yesterday?"

Such comments, casually made, allow children to see that the details recorded in God's word are meaningful to their lives.

We became Christians just a year ago. Our children are teenagers. They haven't accepted Christ yet. Should we try to have devotions with them?

No, not necessarily. The Bible says that "the man without the Spirit does not accept the things that come from the Spirit of God, for they are foolishness to him, and he cannot understand them, because they are spiritually discerned" (1 Corinthians 2:14).

Converse with your teenagers about the things you are

discovering in your new life in Christ and pray for their salvation, but don't force a structured time of spiritual activity, for they wouldn't understand it, nor would it interest them until they, too, have received Christ.

Begin your approach slowly, first by praying before meals, then perhaps by having an occasional family time that is fun and games, but does include a few comments by you regarding your Christian faith. Pray consistently for the salvation of your children, and use varied means at appropriate times to present the gospel to them. Tell them your own testimony, and present the Four Spiritual Laws pamphlet, the Bridge illustration, or another gospel explanation.

Why do other families find time every day to have devotions, but we can't manage it more than once a week?

Meeting together once a week gives your children more spiritual training than if you never met at all. Sometimes we allow our family schedules to become so crowded with good things that the most important thing—spiritual training and interaction—is crowded aside. Both parents should take the time to review individual and family schedules and determine the best time to meet. Usually that will be preceding or following a meal when all family members are at home.

It may be that you simply cannot meet daily. A weekly devotional time may serve for teenagers but is too infrequent to maintain any consistency in teaching younger children. Children will forget from week to week what has been discussed. Use as much flexibility and ingenuity as possible to find times to get together. And if necessary, have devotions with only some of the family members present.

Our children seem bored and restless during our family devotions. We would like them to enjoy our times together and to learn. What are some suggestions we could try?

Restlessness, inattention, and boredom during devotions usually result when the same format is used day after day, or when the material is too immature or too difficult for the child.

When you detect that your family devotions are failing and your children are losing interest, inject something special, something different, something new, but always centered around God and his word. You don't have to present something new and exciting every day, just often enough to keep your children's interest and expectation aroused.

My husband and I both work. We don't have time to prepare anything original or extra. Isn't it enough to read to our children from the Bible and pray a few times a week?

You are to be commended for having the interest to carry on some type of family devotions. However, you will find that planning does not require much of your time—an hour or so at your Christian bookstore two or three times a year and about twenty minutes of planning for a week of devotions.

Devotional planning may take a little more time when you are initially getting underway, but the investment pays off. Hopefully every parent can spare twenty minutes of a 10,080 minute week to give prayer, thought, and preparation to teaching their children the truths of God.

The parents' work schedule should never intrude on the spiritual teaching of the children or influence the amount and content of that teaching.

Isn't it expensive to buy books and materials and some of the extras for family devotions?

No, indeed, it is not. I would estimate the expenses in our family have averaged $20 to $25 per year, a very small portion of the family budget.

We reuse materials, we make liberal use of the public library, we exchange materials with friends, we use the church library, and we try to do things which don't require buying expensive materials.

We haven't tried family devotions yet. Won't our children resent being forced to participate in something that is so much like school?

Are you requiring them to join you in a boring daily drudgery, or are you offering them a delightful, happy, stimulating learning experience? Vary your format, the length of the devotions, the materials, and your location, and you should have interested children. Above all, communicate through words and attitudes your excitement and interest in learning together.

In our family we have three teenagers and a four-year-old. How can we include everyone?

You probably can't. Aim the center of interest toward the older members of the family. Younger children will always grasp something, but older children will automatically turn off if the material is too juvenile for their interests. If the little one appears bored or unhappy, bring something special for him to do or look at during that time.

We have always tried to direct devotions toward the oldest child because we found that our younger children would remain interested. We would then have separate devotions with our child who was several years younger than the other children.

We have had children for ten years and during that time we have started a program of family devotions about a dozen times, but we get so busy and our devotions fizzle out. Should we just give up?

Don't give up! First, review your own convictions. Do you truly feel that spiritual training is the *most* important contribution you can make in your children's lives? It is more significant than their schooling, your neighborhood, their popularity, anything. Ask God to give you that conviction and the dedication and discipline to carry on.

Perhaps you attempted devotions that were too elaborate or lengthy. Simplify your devotional time. Make it brief and to the point. Add an item of interest to the family, then quit. Don't be legalistic about meeting every day, but try as often as possible.

My husband is not a Christian. He thinks Bible reading and prayer are just foolishness. Should I go ahead anyway?

This presents one of the most difficult situations in parenting. Divided interest over spiritual values confuse and bewilder children. If your spouse doesn't directly oppose your teaching the children, by all means, do so, but perhaps when he is not at home so as to reduce any possible ridicule or faultfinding.

Never criticize or degrade your unbelieving spouse to your children. Build up your children's father in their thinking.

Crucial difficulties arise if he specifically forbids you to teach your children. Be patient, live the Christian life before your children, and communicate spiritual truth in short, intimate conversations with each child.

My eleven-year-old son refuses to pray aloud. Should I insist that he do so?

Never force a child to pray. Some children avoid praying aloud even within their own family circle. And other children go through periods when they don't want to pray aloud, but after a few weeks or months they have passed through the phase and are ready to participate again.

The child is not praying to you or for your benefit. Continue to provide a good example of prayer and continue to offer the child an occasional opportunity to pray aloud. And encourage your child to pray privately to the Lord, even though he does not pray aloud in the presence of other people.

When you lead in prayer, do so in simple words and concepts. If you present too sophisticated an example, your child may be intimidated, fearing he cannot measure up to the example you have set.

We live in a neighborhood crowded with children. They often ring our doorbell before we have finished our devotions after dinner, wanting to play with our children. How can we discourage them?

For several evenings, one of the parents could answer the door and explain what you are doing and that your children will be able to play in ten minutes.

Occasionally invite them in to join you. We have often had

our dinner table crowded with little faces eager to join in what we were doing. And our children are usually more attentive when guests or friends join us.

If your devotions are interesting and enjoyable, your children won't mind delaying their playtime for awhile to be with you in a pleasant spiritual learning experience.

We have enrolled our children in a Christian school. Won't it be redundant to have devotions at home when they have had Bible class during the day?

The Bible teaches that parents are primarily responsible for the spiritual training of their children. If our children don't experience Bible teaching from us, we will have neglected the most important part of our relationship with them. Consider the Christian school as supplemental to what you give your children at home, not the reverse.

12 Keys to Continuing

ANY PARENT WOULD be discouraged to hear comments like, "Dad, why don't we have Bible reading anymore?" "Do you remember when we used to sing together? That was fun." "I wish you would tell us Bible stories now."

Such remarks cut sharply into the conscience of parents who want to maintain consistent, successful family devotions. Every serious Christian parent wants to be the major contributing factor in the spiritual development of his children.

Jim and Avis practiced daily devotions when their three children were small. About the time they entered their teens, Jim accepted a job that required a great deal of travel. Avis became so busy with the children and their hectic schedules that when Jim was absent she let devotions slide. When Jim was at home, the family seemed to be so busy that they just didn't gather for devotions.

When their oldest child left for college, Avis asked him to reminisce about his happy times at home.

"One thing I liked best was family Bible time," he said. "We used to have some fun times. It's sure been a long time since we did that."

Jim and Avis felt stricken by his answer and resolved to start once again with the two children left in their home. They found only two days a week when they could meet, but they decided to make the most of those times.

Many conditions cause parents to abandon plans for family devotions.

- Too busy a schedule
- Lack of planning
- Family members with conflicting schedules
- Lack of success
- Rebellion on the part of one child
- Decreasing motivation
- Lack of imagination and ideas

The single most important key to maintaining a continuing program of family devotions is parental conviction. Unless parents are convinced that their spiritual influence and teaching are of utmost importance to their children, the family devotional time will falter and eventually fail.

Children may raise objections or show no interest from time to time, but their attitudes cannot be a controlling influence in the decision to go on.

Parents wouldn't think of asking their children if they want to continue in school. They know that school is a necessary privilege for children. Similarly, spiritual training cannot be an option. That certainty is based on Scripture. "Fathers, do not exasperate your children; instead, bring them up in the training and instruction of the Lord" (Ephesians 6:4). "These commandments that I give you today are to be upon your hearts. Impress them on your children. Talk about them when you sit at home and when you walk along the road, when you lie down and when you get up" (Deuteronomy 6:6-7).

Not only should conviction control the parents, but also personal practice. Children need to see their parents reading the Bible and praying at times other than family devotions. When I was a girl I often saw my parents reading the Bible and praying. Even today when my father visits our home, I appreciate seeing him reading his Bible.

Conviction and personal practice are the two essential elements for ongoing family devotions. Many other things supplement your teaching—books, visual aids, records, and pictures. But they are only aids and cannot provide the sustaining motivation to keep family devotions going for months and years.

Ask God for the conviction you need and an understanding of the importance of your personal spiritual leadership and teaching. And then resolve to read your Bible and pray on a daily basis. God wants to fellowship with you and speak to you as well as to your family.

Personal devotions undergird family devotions. In fact, the two reinforce one another. Parents who maintain a consistent time of personal fellowship with God will more likely continue successful family devotions.

When devotions have become firmly established, what else keeps them going? Four other ingredients provide support for continuing devotions.

Planning. Many parents avoid an attempt at creativity in their family devotions, fearing it will require expensive, time-consuming preparations.

You can give your devotional time new meaning and sparkle if you spend just a few minutes a day, or twenty to thirty minutes a week assembling, organizing, and planning the time. Gather everything you plan to use, such as Bible, prayer list, visual aids, prizes, and so on. That way you don't have to say, "It's time for devotions. Who knows where the Bible is?" or "What shall we read today?"

You will find it helpful to plan ahead for two weeks of devotional times. That will give you enough time to plan an extended series of Bible studies or special activities. Good preparation also enables you to start every day without a last-minute rush to find something to do. Your preparation takes only a little time and pays dividends in more interesting devotions and more satisfied children.

Brevity. "Cut it short." Apply the rule—the younger the child, the shorter the devotions. A toddler can tolerate, at most, about five minutes of concentration. Besides, you have years to teach him. He doesn't need to know it all by the time he is five years old. Older children will appreciate extended devotions, but never aim for the maximum possible time and risk losing their attention.

Whenever possible, leave the child feeling that he wants more, that he wasn't quite finished listening and participating. Children should leave family devotions with the thought, *Isn't there more?* instead of, *Finally, it's over!*

I visited in a home where family devotions were conducted once a week on Sunday afternoon. Since the devotions were infrequent, the parents tried to maximize the time by making it lengthy. After a long Scripture reading, the father produced questions for discussion. If the children couldn't answer the questions, the father reread the passage until he heard the right answer. During the entire time the children, most of them in their elementary school years, wiggled, yawned, sighed, and punched each other.

Eventually, the father asked for prayer requests. Then came a long prayer by both parents, during which time two of the children slid off their chairs, nestled comfortably on the carpet, and punctuated the prayers with their gentle snores.

What went wrong? The parents included the right ingredients for an effective time of family worship and fellowship, but overshot the time by a wide margin. A short time together would have proven much more effective in arousing and sustaining the children's interest.

Very small children one to three years old should have devotions lasting only a few minutes, preschool children five to ten minutes, elementary school children about ten to fifteen minutes, and teens from five to thirty minutes.

The less children participate, the shorter the devotions need to be. If your devotions include your children in some active way, you are safe in extending the time and still keeping their interest. If you are using visual aids, you can hold their attention for a longer period than if you are just reading and talking.

Children offer obvious clues when they are restless, bored, or disinterested. Their feet shuffle, their eyes stare, they scratch where it doesn't itch, they yawn, sprawl, sigh, and kick. So if their attention has vanished, why continue?

Learn to keep things moving briskly. Have all the materials

ready, read fast, move quickly from reading to singing to prayer to special activities.

Too often we hear children say,

- Can we quit now?
- Mom, can I go play with my friends?
- When are we going to be done?
- This is boring.

What we really want to hear is,

- Don't stop yet, Dad.
- Hey, I really like this.
- I didn't know the Bible said that.
- Let's do more tomorrow.

Occasionally lengthen the time you spend together, perhaps on a leisurely Saturday morning, a Sunday evening, or on a vacation trip. During an extended time, include additional stimulating materials and activities. An occasional longer devotional time will give children a sense of the personal benefit and pleasure that results from prolonged periods in God's presence and will serve to draw the family together.

One summer our family spent a few days camping in the mountains. On a chilly evening we sat around a crackling campfire, bundled in coats, idly toasting marshmallows.

During the preceding weeks we had been emphasizing God's desire for us to have thankful spirits. Now as we huddled close around the fire we read a Bible story, then began in short sentence prayers to give thanks to God. Some would say that the chemistry of the situation was right. More likely the Spirit of God was working in our little group, as we were drawn together in an awareness of God's presence and his goodness to us.

No one was eager to leave and we stayed together talking quietly of spiritual things until the sun faded completely and the stars glittered above us. Such memorable times happen only occasionally, but bring a lasting zest to everyday devotions.

Variety. "Keep them guessing." Do your children know precisely what you will do each day during your devotional time? Are you as predictable as the rising sun? Can they anticipate an occasional surprise? Do they look forward to the unexpected? Do you plan an occasional exciting, interesting, or enjoyable devotion?

Perhaps you balk at the suggestion to have fun during devotions. Maybe you feel that any spiritual activity should be solemn, hushed, and reverent.

The Bible speaks often of the joy, rejoicing, and delight to be found in the presence of the Lord. 2 Samuel 6 records King David's reaction to the return of the ark of the Lord to Jerusalem. He experienced so much joy that he danced and leaped in the streets. Later when discussing his behavior with his wife, Michal, he insisted, "I will celebrate before the Lord" (2 Samuel 6:21).

Some may draw the line at including a dance program as part of your family devotions. But do allow your children to approach God with you in a spirit of joy and delight.

Adults who have fellowshipped with God for years know the pleasure of the surprises he has for us in Scripture and prayer. Have you ever been reading along in Scripture and suddenly a great truth or promise leaped out at you? For days, weeks, or even months following that time, the special truth came rushing back to capture your thoughts and delight your heart. Have you been praying when suddenly you were overwhelmed with the realization that the God of all creation was, at that moment, taking pleasure in your fellowship?

We do want our children to experience the delight of a living, personal relationship with God. When we use variety in our devotions, we come a little closer to giving them that sense of joy. Certainly we hold their attention for a longer period, and that alone pays rewards. What can you vary in devotions?

- Use different materials to present Scripture.
- Change your location. There is no special benefit in staying at the dining room table or sitting in the living room. Go outside, kneel around a bed, sit on the floor.

- Change the format of prayer. Change prayer positions—sit, stand, kneel, lie down, walk.
- Let one of your children plan and lead devotions.
- Invite a guest to share his testimony.
- Vary the time of day you meet.
- Skip a day (not too often).
- Meet twice on one day.
- Climb in the car, go to the park, and sit under a tree.
- Spend the entire time praying.
- Spend the entire time singing.

Children don't need to be aware of the reasons for specific changes and variations. If their interest is captured and their learning increased, that is enough.

Plan on some deviation from your standard routine about once a week or once every two weeks. Your children will anticipate the changes you announce.

Flexibility. "Roll with the punches." Always be willing to make changes in family devotions. Flexibility and variety go hand in hand to bring a freshness and enjoyment to the time together.

Flexibility provides a protection against legalism. Structure provides a framework to keep going, but structure must never be an end in itself. Many situations will arise when you must change plans and timing. Although such times will happen, we don't need to feel guilty or frustrated by such events. We can carry on our devotional plans with a minimum of disruption.

What kinds of situations demand flexibility?

- Illness of various family members
- Traveling parents
- Teens' activities and schedules
- An important long-distance phone call
- Conflicting school schedules
- Special events at school

A few years ago we had one child in elementary school, another in junior high school, a third in senior high school, and the oldest in college although living at home. For a time we found ourselves quite frustrated, as we tried to gather them all together at some point in the day.

We finally concluded it just couldn't be done, so we picked a time when the majority would be there. We found it worked quite well. Some of the children were with us every day, while one or two could come only a few times each week.

We have found that flexibility increases our creativity and planning. When we know we will have to make allowances for other situations and events, we can do so with a minimum of disruption and frustration. If we have to skip a time or two, we make an effort to be well prepared with interesting ideas for the times we are together.

When your children are tiny, you control their time and schedules. But as they grow older, school, church, and sports activities invade family life. You must adjust to those additional inputs.

Be prepared to adapt your daily and weekly routine to accommodate minor interruptions and long-term schedule changes. If you have captivating devotions, your children will regard the interruptions with regret rather than relief at the welcome release from a boring encounter. They will be eager to resume at the earliest opportunity.

Conviction, planning, brevity, flexibility, and variety combine to keep family devotions going, regardless of interruptions and frustrations. And those consistent family devotions will pay off in children who love God and grow into adults who revere and serve him.

Now is the time for personal application. No amount of teaching or persuasion can make family devotions work. Only you can do that. But it requires a decision to begin where you are with what you have.

This book suggests only a beginning; you must be the finisher. Will it be easy? No. Will it be worth the effort? Yes! Family devotions can be the greatest investment you will make in your children. The burden rests on your shoulders, and on God's. He is the great teacher. He will enable you to help your children grow deep spiritual roots that will hold in any storm.

God will give you the will and the discipline needed to lead and to feed your children a balanced diet of spiritual food. He will strengthen your desire and teach you, too. He has given you the privilege of being a parent. And with that privilege he promises to guide your life and the lives of your children.

94932